Write on Kew

London's inspiring new literary festival

Wendy Cope Esther Freud
Dan Cruickshank Claire Tomalin
Margaret Atwood Michael Morpurgo
Melvyn Bragg Bill Bryson Judith Kerr
Louis de Bernières Simon Armitage
William Fiennes Thomas Pakenham

Royal Botanic Gardens
Kew

24 – 28 September
kew.org/write-on-kew
⊖ Kew Gardens
⇌ Kew Bridge

Write on Kew
A literary festival at Kew Gardens

Everything

LITUAKE

"LITQUAKE IS TO
THE LITERARY
WORLD WHAT
SOUTH BY
SOUTHWEST IS
TO THE MUSIC
INDUSTRY OR
SUNDANCE IS TO
INDEPENDENT
FILM."
—*SAN FRANCISCO
EXAMINER*

**LITQUAKE
FESTIVAL**
SAN FRANCISCO
OCTOBER 9–17, 2015

LIT CAST
PODCASTS

**KIDQUAKE &
TEENQUAKE**
YOUTH
PROGRAMS

**MASTER
CLASS
MIXERS**
WRITING
SEMINARS

EPICENTER
AUTHOR
CONVERSATIONS

**LIT
CRAWLS**
IN NINE
CITIES

HEADQUARTERED IN SAN FRANCISCO | LITQUAKE.ORG | LITCRAWL.ORG

BBC Proms

17 JULY – 12 SEPTEMBER 2015
ROYAL ALBERT HALL

The world's greatest classical music festival
92 CONCERTS OVER 61 DAYS

This year, download the BBC Proms Guide app for just £2.99

BOOK NOW
SEATS FROM £7.50*
STANDING TICKETS £5.00 ON THE DAY

For full details of the 2015 Proms season visit **bbc.co.uk/proms**
or call **0845 401 5040†**

Sign up for our newsletter at bbc.co.uk/proms
Join us on Facebook and Tumblr or follow us on Instagram and Twitter #bbcproms

GRANTA

12 Addison Avenue, London W11 4QR | email editorial@granta.com
To subscribe go to granta.com, or call 020 8955 7011 (free phone 0500 004 033)
in the United Kingdom, 845-267-3031 (toll-free 866-438-6150) in the United States

ISSUE 132: SUMMER 2015

PUBLISHER AND EDITOR	Sigrid Rausing
MANAGING EDITOR	Yuka Igarashi
ONLINE AND POETRY EDITOR	Rachael Allen
DESIGNER	Daniela Silva
EDITORIAL ASSISTANTS	Luke Neima, Francisco Vilhena
SUBSCRIPTIONS	David Robinson
PUBLICITY	Aidan O'Neill
TO ADVERTISE CONTACT	Kate Rochester, katerochester@granta.com
FINANCE	Morgan Graver
SALES AND MARKETING	Iain Chapple, Katie Hayward
IT MANAGER	Mark Williams
PRODUCTION ASSOCIATE	Sarah Wasley
PROOFS	David Atkinson, Francine Brody, Amber Dowell, Katherine Fry, Vimbai Shire
CONTRIBUTING EDITORS	Daniel Alarcón, Anne Carson, Mohsin Hamid, Isabel Hilton, Michael Hofmann, A.M. Homes, Janet Malcolm, Adam Nicolson, Edmund White

THE OLD VIC

FUTURE CONDITIONAL
By TAMSIN OGLESBY

1 SEPT - 3 OCT 2015

THE HAIRY APE
17 OCT - 21 NOV 2015

By EUGENE O'NEILL

DR. SEUSS'S THE LORAX
2 DEC 2015 - 16 JAN 2016

Adapted by DAVID GREIG

PRINCIPAL PARTNER ROYAL BANK OF CANADA

THE MASTER BUILDER
By HENRIK IBSEN
New adaptation by DAVID HARE

JEKYLL & HYDE
A NEW DANCE THRILLER by DREW McONIE

THE CARETAKER
By HAROLD PINTER

GROUNDHOG DAY
Book by DANNY RUBIN
Music & lyrics by TIM MINCHIN

OUR COMMUNITY PRODUCTION

RISE

PRINCIPAL PARTNER

PREVIEWS PARTNER

pwc

0844 871 7628
oldvictheatre.com

RBC

Royal Bank of Canada

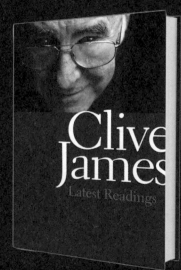

CONTENTS

7/2015

Introduction

When my son was two and a half, in the spring of the year 2000, I bought a Cavalier King Charles spaniel puppy. We had driven down to Lewes to see it, to a breeder who was, I remember, preoccupied by the ghost of her husband. He left her messages in the kitchen by moving a tin of biscuits or the jar of Marmite. We drank milky tea and talked about his absence. Later Daniel, my son, sat on the floor of the kennels and held the tiny puppy that was to be ours, then only a few weeks old.

Fifteen years later, Leo was very old. His hind legs dragged, and he was blind and deaf, though to what degree was hard to tell. I came back from a radio show in Sweden to find him with a deep open blister on his paw – a blister that, this time, was unlikely to heal.

We called the vet the next day. She came with an assistant. We brought his bed out and I held him, feeling his heart beating. They shaved his hind leg. For a moment I wanted to stop them, to protect him from what was about to happen, but I didn't. And then his heart stopped.

The moment between life and death was almost imperceptible. The ease of that transition was enviable and yet also shocking. We buried him wrapped in a sheet, but for a while beforehand he lay on the sheet, in the sun. We lay on the grass next to him. His fur was moving in the wind so that he seemed still alive. Archaic thoughts of the horrors of the cold, dark grave came to me, along with an obsessive – and unexpected – conviction that he was not really dead. We tried, and failed, to close his eyes. The line between the human and the non-human seemed so fine – I felt a sense of existential confusion about this meeting of possession, love and death.

None of this had ever struck me as problematic before. I grew up with animals, and therefore with death. My father would shoot our old dogs (and later his old laptops). But the ownership of sentient beings, and the power possession gives you, seems to me now a graver matter than I believed then.

This issue of *Granta* is about possession, in many different guises. Oliver Bullough writes about the surreal aftermath of the revolution in Ukraine, and the situation in Crimea following the Russian annexation. Kerry Howley, who has written a book on cage fighting, describes giving birth in the context of her belief in the value of the fight, and of endurance. Marc Bojanowski's story, 'This is New', shows how a single moment of impatience leading to a violent gesture can destroy a career. We are, in that sense, at the mercy of our ids. Our superegos try their best to remain in control but they often fail – and perhaps the destruction of a career could in fact be justified with reference to the psychoanalytic theory of the unconscious. If the id can take control once it can do so again.

Bella Pollen's disturbing memoir piece is also about the power of the mind: she describes her waking nightmares, of being sexually possessed by an incubus. There is a scientific explanation for these things, but even so it is an anthropological riddle how similar the incubus phenomenon turns out to be across cultures and eras. Why is it that humanity seems to invent and reinvent the same male or female nightmare demon?

Poet Molly Brodak's memoir about her father, a Polish-American gambler and failed bank robber, is unexpectedly framed by the aftermath of war. He was born in a displaced persons camp in 1945, and the family ended up in Detroit. Brodak finds the now derelict house they stayed in as refugees: 'The sky can be so solid gray in Michigan, like wet concrete, churning without breaking for days. Under it, this home, sinking into the earth, the earth digesting its own paradox, in silence.'

Possession takes many forms, and at the heart of it is death and dereliction, invasion and submission. Nothing can be still, as poet Rae Armantrout writes. Possession and loss are intertwined. ∎

Sigrid Rausing

from *Feud*
Maidan, Kiev, 18 February 2014

AFTER MAIDAN

Oliver Bullough

1. Kiev, April 2014

Central Kiev was dirty and sooty from the revolution two months before. The barricades blocked traffic: great heaped piles of cobblestones and ash, rusted wire and burnt tyres, shields, trash, home-made tank traps of rails welded together into crude tripods. Bottles of petrol, packed into milk crates and stoppered with rags, lay forgotten among the rubbish. Protesters, with their green army-surplus tents, still occupied the Maidan, the square in the centre of town.

The tents and protesters alike were frayed, though: a shanty town of people looking increasingly as if they had nowhere else to go. The city government tolerated them for now. It had better things to do, like trying to get its headquarters back. City Hall bore a scrawled legend – HEADQUARTERS OF THE REVOLUTION – and scruffy men in camouflage stood by the door. They said they were guarding the revolution, but locals had begun to wrinkle their noses a little when they picked their way past.

I walked through the encampment, past the last barricade to the end of Khreschatyk. I passed some burnt-out cars and an armoured personnel carrier with tourists posing in front of it, and began up the hill. To the left was the old Dynamo Stadium, scene of some legendary performances over the years by Ukraine's most famous football club. On my right was a queue: a few hundred Ukrainians were waiting in the pale sunshine to enter the National Art Museum.

I had an appointment, so I walked past them up the steps and went to find Natalia Shostak. She was twenty-five and had worked at the museum as a guide for three years, but these last few months of mayhem had upended her life and her work. The museum's paintings were gone, hidden for the duration of the turmoil. The ground-floor galleries were exhibiting a weirder haul: treasures found by the revolutionaries at President Viktor Yanukovich's abandoned palace.

The palace, Mezhyhirya, had become a tourist attraction. Ordinary Ukrainians flocked there to marvel at the vast log-built main building, the fountains, the waterfalls, the golf course, the statues, the exotic pheasants, the reconstructed Greek temple, the dining room shaped like a galleon, the life-size marble horse painted with a Tuscan landscape. It was a temple of tastelessness, a cathedral of kitsch, the epitome of excess. Enterprising locals rented bikes to visitors. There was no other way to see the whole site without becoming exhausted.

Shostak spoke beautiful English, but seemed lost for words. How to conduct a tour when the objects were shown with the intention of provoking revulsion? Was it even art? And if so, how? How would one articulate the concept behind this exhibition?

When the revolutionaries arrived at Mezhyhirya, they sealed the doors to prevent looting. They had found boxes and boxes of treasure in the garages: an Aladdin's cave of golden goods. They called the museum's curators to take it all away before it got damaged, to preserve it for the nation.

'The revolutionaries thought all of this was very precious, but the museum's specialists thought it was just kitsch, a combination of uncombinable things. Very few of these works have artistic or cultural value,' Shostak explained. So the curators displayed it like junk in a flea market: piles of gold-painted candlesticks, walls full of portraits of the president. There were statues of Greek gods and ivory carved into intricate oriental pagodas. There were icons, dozens of icons, antique rifles and swords and axes. There were certificates declaring Yanukovich to be 'hunter of the year', and certificates announcing that a star had been named in his honour, and another for his wife.

Ukraine is perhaps the only country on earth that, after being looted for years by a greed-drunk kleptocrat, would repurpose his and his cronies' and admirers' execrable knick-knacks as immersive conceptual art. No one present seemed sure whether to be proud or ashamed of that fact.

The curators' stated aim was to create not just a composite portrait of the former president (his greed, his vanity, his crudeness) but also of the society that elected him. The fact that this appalling man was a product of Ukraine was an uncomfortable message for many Ukrainians, and many chose to ignore it. 'The principle is not to show people what is valuable. This is a mass of stuff to show how tasteless Yanukovich and his surroundings were. But most people are interested in what is valuable,' Shostak said sadly.

I understood why she was unhappy about it. It would have been lovely for everyone to have entered the gallery with the same lofty meta-appreciation of kitsch-as-cultural-signifier that the curators possessed. But that was asking a lot; it was certainly asking too much of me. I found it irresistible to marvel at quite how much money had been spent on such mediocre objects, how many pearls had been strewn before this very boorish swine.

There was an ancient tome, displayed in a vitrine, with a sign declaring it to have been a present from the tax ministry. It was a copy of *Apostol*, the first book ever printed in Ukraine, of which perhaps only a hundred copies still exist. Why had the tax ministry decided that this was an appropriate gift for the president? How could it afford it? No one knew. In a pile of trashy ceramics was an exquisite Picasso vase. Among the modern icons there was at least one from the fourteenth century, with the flat perspective that has inspired Orthodox devotion for a millennium. On display tables, next to a portrait of Yanukovich executed in amber, and another one picked out in seeds harvested from a variety of Ukrainian cereal crops, were nineteenth-century Russian landscapes worth millions of dollars. A display cabinet housed a steel hammer and sickle, which had once been a present to Joseph Stalin from the Ukrainian Communist Party. How did it get into Yanukovich's garage? Perhaps the president had nowhere else to put it.

Room followed room. It was like being led around an IKEA-sized antique shop, where nothing was for sale. A whole room was full of pictures of women, unclothed, standing around in the open air surrounded by men, clothed. Another was full of weapons and stuffed animals. By the last room, both Shostak and I were exhausted. Neither of us had the energy to remark on a flayed crocodile stuck to the wall, or to wonder at the display cabinets full of even more weapons. There were eleven rifles, four swords, twelve pistols and a spear – or those are the numbers I wrote down. Looking at my photographs now, there seem to have been many more than that, so I'm not sure my notes from the time are reliable. I felt slightly delirious, as if I'd engaged in a long discussion with someone whose viewpoint I could not, no matter how hard I tried, comprehend.

The public kept coming. By the time I escaped back into the spring sunshine, the queue at the gate was even longer. The people waiting looked jolly, edging slowly forward to vanish behind the museum's pebble-dashed pediment. When they emerged again, they looked different – ashen, sick. By the final door was a book for comments. Someone had written: 'How much can one man need? Horror. I feel nauseated.'

I walked back through the government district, across to Institutska Street, then downhill again, under the bridge to the Maidan. This is where snipers shot dozens of protesters – by now immortalised in street portraits as the Heavenly Hundred – in the act of slaughter that brought about the end of the Yanukovich regime.

A crew of four street cleaners with a JCB digger was picking at the barricades, chucking tyres into the front loader, scooping up ash by the shovelful. They didn't seem very enthusiastic, but then the task ahead of them was daunting. The barricades were huge. A revolutionary in camouflage sat in an open-sided tent and watched, without making any effort either to obstruct or to help. Passers-by took photographs. Kiev was getting back to normal.

2. Sukholuchya, July 2014

Three months later, I was a passenger in a car driven fast through a Ukrainian forest. Ukraine has three kinds of road. The first type runs between cities: busy and relatively well-maintained dual carriageways dotted with advertising. The second kind runs between towns and villages: poorly maintained and deeply potholed, frequented by Ladas and minibuses. The third kind you find inside cities: lined with parked cars, which unpredictably reverse out in front of you, potholed too, sometimes cobbled, infested with policemen.

This road was like none of them. It was smooth as a pool table and black as the eight ball, edged with lines as straight and as white as the birch trees outside. It was also deserted. We didn't see another car for half an hour. It felt like we had passed out of time – we could keep driving forever, and never reach the end. The sun beat down, casting mirages onto the tarmac ahead. It was the kind of warm that Ukraine gets during a long and dusty summer. Harvesting weather, beer-for-lunch weather, as gold and as blue as the Ukrainian flag.

Anton was driving. A friend had told me about Anton, about an extraordinary secret he had discovered, and had given me his number. Everyone knew everyone in Kiev; everyone was happy to talk, to take me anywhere I wanted to go. Anton had run his own IT company before joining the AutoMaidan, the motorised wing of the revolution. He loved to drive, and he loved having passengers.

There was a gate.

'What's this, Anton?' his mother asked.

'Shhh, Mum,' he said. This had been his response to every question she had asked since we left Kiev. I was not entirely sure why she was with us. Anton had not introduced us, and I was left wondering whether I was supposed to ignore her too. I had adopted a compromise: I never actually said anything to her, but smiled encouragingly whenever she spoke. Like all compromises, however, I suspect it satisfied neither of them. It certainly wasn't making me any happier. The second car held the three other members of our party: Yelena and Sergei, a refugee couple from the town of Sloviansk in Eastern Ukraine, and their daughter Natalia. They had come for something to do. Time was something they had plenty of since separatists had taken over their town and they had fled with what they could fit into the boot of their car.

Anton stepped off the road into the undergrowth, rustled around and came out with a key. He held it up. 'The key to paradise,' he said, with a lopsided smile. He unlocked the gate, got back behind the wheel and drove through. Sergei's car followed. Anton locked up again, and we moved on, along the immaculate surface of the abandoned road.

To our right we could see, glimmering, the surface of the Kiev Reservoir, where the dammed waters of the Dnieper swell into an inland sea dotted with reed beds. We crossed a causeway over a narrow pond by a small boathouse with a dock. Ducks fussed around their wooden houses on little floating islands. We drove through the trees and pulled up at a turning circle in front of a two-storey log mansion.

'Are we here?' Anton's mother asked.

'Shhh, Mum,' he said.

This was Yanukovich's other palace, the Sukholuchya hunting lodge, where the president had brought his friends to drink, to shoot, to party, to have sex. Its existence had been a rumour before the revolution. Everyone knew there was a closely guarded road into the forest, but the only people who knew where it led weren't saying. Then, in February 2014, the president fled his capital. No one was in charge, and anything was possible; so Anton got into his car and drove down that immaculate road. He had brought his daughter and, giddy with revolution, they greeted the policemen guarding the gate. Open up, they said, the people are here, or words to that effect.

The policemen gave them the key, and Anton drove on.

He pulled up in front of the mansion, and looked out over the grounds dotted with mature trees. There was a chapel and an open-sided summer house with a barbecue. The ground sloped gently down to a marina for yachts. The staff came out to meet him, and he told them the revolution had won. Their master, Yanukovich, was gone, and the hunting lodge belonged to the people.

Now Anton opened the door of the mansion, and we filed in. He had changed nothing: the long dining table and its eighteen overstuffed chairs were left as he had found them, as was the heated marble massage table, the nine televisions (two of them in the en-suite bathrooms, opposite the toilets, at sitting-down height), the low-grade sub-Impressionist nudes – the kind of thing Renoir might have painted if he'd moved into soft porn. The floor was of highly polished boards, tropical hardwood, the walls squared softwood logs, deliberately left unfinished, yellow as sesame seeds. There were no books.

Yelena and Natalia set off on their own, apparently determined to photograph each other on every piece of soft furnishing in the place. It was going to take them a while. Anton took me from room to room, pulling out the karaoke machine, opening up the plunge pool, telling me the story of how he ended up running the place. It was still technically the property of Yanukovich's hunting club, owned via a British shell company, but Anton had taken over the bank accounts. He used the money to pay a skeleton staff charged with keeping the place clean and the lawns cut. He still hoped the new government would create a mechanism to return these mansions (this was just one of many) to the people, to undo the mad kleptocracy that had swept over Ukraine since the end of communism.

He had always intended his control of the Sukholuchya hunting lodge to be temporary, but time had passed, and nothing had happened. The snows melted; spring came. The swallows flew back from Africa, and built their mud nests under the mansion's eaves. They laid and hatched eggs, fed their chicks on the flies that dart in millions over the water. The chicks ate, grew to full size, fledged and took flight themselves. We saw them perched untidily along the mansion's ridgeline, ready to head south. And still Anton held the keys.

'What do you think I should do with this place?' he asked as he searched for the key to the chapel.

It was an interesting question. The place was secluded and peaceful. It had a shooting range, hunting grounds, a jacuzzi, several outdoor pavilions for impromptu picnics as well as the finest driveway in Europe, if not the world: all the facilities you might want if you were rich and powerful. But it was too small to host conferences, and too big and remote to be any normal person's house. I suggested that he could organise a lottery, open to everyone: Buy a ticket! Win the chance to live like a president for a week! Anton laughed. It was as good an idea as any, though he imagined one of the officials of the new government would end up getting their hands on the place. He had already beaten off a couple of attempts.

Sergei came out and joined us, and we speculated about what Yanukovich was doing now, in exile in Russia, cut off from his luxurious palaces, watching his homeland fall apart.

'He probably misses all this. He's a refugee like us, after all,' said Sergei.

'Not exactly like you,' said Anton's mum.

'Shhh, Mum,' said Anton.

3. Kiev, August 2014

If you want to go to Kiev, don't bother with hotels; find a flat on the Internet. The local currency has collapsed since the revolution, and you can rent a nice central place for what it used to cost to get a single room on the outskirts. I was renting from a woman called Olyona, an artist, whose flat I found on a rental website. This is Ukraine, however, and no one obeys the rules, so she immediately looked me up on Facebook and proposed that I pay 20 per cent less, in cash, when I arrived, thus circumventing the website and depriving it of its fee.

She was away when I arrived, and a friend of hers, Sergei, let me in. He wore a singlet and the kind of shorts worn by basketball players, though he was at least a foot too short for the role. He chain-smoked roll-ups, and was about to go to California. He had taken part in the revolution in some way that he wasn't keen to elaborate on, and had been arrested by the police back in January.

After Yanukovich fled, the police had left Sergei alone. Now, however, they were after him again. 'Time has passed, and they reckon they can get away with it,' he said. We were sitting on the balcony, where Olyona had placed an armchair and a hammock. He was planning to claim asylum in the United States, he said, and to stay there for good. The next morning I noticed that he'd left his tobacco, lighter and papers on the table, and I felt sorry for him: on his own in a strange country with no smokes.

At the bottom of the hill, the Maidan was full of people collecting money for the army, which was fighting Russian-supplied separatists, and was hopelessly outgunned. The donated money went towards food, flak jackets, medicines – anything to give the soldiers a better chance of survival. There were beggars too. I gave one of them Sergei's tobacco, though he didn't acknowledge it.

A couple of nights later a friend was in a gay club when the police raided it. They came mob-handed, a dozen officers with guns and bulletproof vests, looking for drugs, they said. The officers made everyone lie flat on the floor with their arms and legs out – a constellation of starfish wearing the most fashionable clothes in Kiev – until the club owners managed to reach an agreement on the sum of money the police would accept in order to go away. 'That's Ukraine now,' my friend said. 'You spend the day raising money for soldiers who don't have flak jackets but need them; then at night you have to give money to policemen who have flak jackets but don't need them.'

Olyona had told me that she normally holidayed in Crimea with her family. Russia had annexed Crimea that March, though, so she had gone to the dacha instead. Hundreds of thousands of Ukrainians had done likewise, leaving Crimea's beaches empty, and those Crimeans who were orientated towards Kiev cut off and isolated. Among them were the Tatars, Crimea's indigenous community, who had been whittled down to just 15 per cent of the peninsula's population by Stalin's mass deportation in 1944, by war, by emigration and immigration. The Tatars blamed Moscow for their nation's near-extinction, and did not welcome being ruled by Russia once more. They looked to Kiev to help them, but Kiev had its hands full, and no help came.

The Tatars' political centre in Kiev was now an office just off the Maidan. This is where Mustafa Jemilev spent his days. He and his family had been victims of the mass deportation, and he'd grown up in exile in Uzbekistan. He was now seventy, and had led the Crimean Tatar national movement for most of the last fifty years: first as a young student and author of samizdat history essays; then as a political prisoner, a hunger striker in the Soviet camps; and then as a free man, who brought his nation back from Stalinist exile in 1989. Now that Russia was in charge, he was in exile once more, identified as an extremist and banned from Crimea.

I entered a ragged and dirty courtyard, and walked through an arch to Jemilev's office on the first floor. It was in a converted apartment, and his room may once have been a child's bedroom. He sat behind a broad, dark, wood-effect desk, a television playing silently on the wall above him. By the time he was two, nearly half of all Crimean Tatars had died. The privations of his childhood had permanently stunted his growth. He was tiny and wizened, his face deeply lined by his experiences. He looked kind, wise and thoughtful. He looked gentle, sardonic and watchful. He did not look extreme. Nonetheless, Putin had almost spat when describing Jemilev's opposition to Russia's annexation of Crimea: 'We will not work with those who speculate on the past's problems, make it their profession and livelihood, and use past problems for their own PR. We will not work with these people,' he said, when asked why Jemilev was not allowed home.

Jemilev looked amused when he recalled these words, but then he pretty much always looks amused. When he smiles, the right side of his mouth rises first. His heavy eyebrows lift too, and the bags under his eyes smooth a little. He uses his cigarette as a prop, an aid to thought, rolling it between his thumb and index finger, to the top and down again. He had done a lot of thinking during our chat: this was his seventh cigarette he had pulled out of the pack. The Formica of the desk was spotted with tobacco flakes and fragments of ash. His answers and my questions were punctuated with deep, productive coughs that shook his whole body.

'If for your whole life you've fought for an idea, for your principles, you've sacrificed your whole youth to it, and you hear some promises...' He paused and lit the cigarette, inhaled deeply. His throat was scratchy; it had been a long day. 'That would render my whole life null and void, and for what?'

Putin had told the world that he had had no choice but to annex Crimea, that Crimea was sacred to the Russians. Perhaps he had believed it, but his voice had none of the yearning that Jemilev's had when he described not being able to see his ancestral village of Ay-Serez. 'I want to be buried there,' he said, with a slight twitch of his mouth. There was little amusement on his face now.

4. Simferopol, March 2014

I had last seen Crimea in March. It was just a few days before Putin announced he would annex it: the first annexation in Europe since 1945. Mysterious, well-armed vigilantes had appeared on the streets; the local parliament had voted to organise a referendum on joining

OLIVER BULLOUGH

Russia. These were strange, underwater days, and nothing made sense. Unidentified troops closed neighbourhoods and blockaded military bases. Putin denied that they came from Russia, but they drove around in Russian military vehicles, and Russian flags sprouted in their wake: Aquafresh tricolours on building after building.

The men in uniform: were they Russian soldiers pretending to be volunteers? Or were they volunteers pretending to be Russian soldiers pretending to be volunteers? Or were they genuinely volunteers? Or were they maniacs taking advantage of the chaos, who'd nick my camera if I went too close? A lot depended on not getting that calculation wrong, not least the future of my camera, since there was no way my travel insurance would honour a claim I made from here. The think tanks called it a hybrid war, as if it were some kind of biological curiosity, an armoured mule, but that didn't capture it. It wasn't a war at all; it was something else, something nasty, dishonest and unpredictable.

There were rumours of crosses appearing on the doors of Tatars' houses, of Muslims being marked for retribution, of Russian speakers hunted by Ukrainian death squads. When I wanted to find sense of it all one evening, I drove out to Tatar neighbourhoods, where groups of young men stood around fires burning in oil drums, like a movie scene of Harlem in the 1980s. They kept their heads when all about them were losing theirs, spectacularly.

Most Tatars live apart from the rest of Crimea's residents – a legacy of their deportation by Stalin in 1944. They were only allowed home at the very end of the Soviet period, and never got their old houses back. Pre-1944, they had lived in villages tucked into the folds of the hills along the coast. Now, they live wherever they had found land, normally on the edges of Russian-speaking towns, in places no one else wanted. In the early 1990s, when the Tatars first came back, these shanty towns looked like bits of the Third World dumped in Europe. With time, however, with hard work, dedication and community, the neighbourhoods developed solid structures, nice houses, shops and businesses. Their streets were still unpaved, though, and often unlit, a legacy of the fact that the local government had never wanted the Tatars to come home in the first place. The Russians called this spontaneous acquisition of property 'self-seizure'; the Tatars called it 'self-return'.

The young Tatar men standing round the fires were guards, assigned by their communities to keep an eye on who was coming in and out. These teenagers were geopolitically far-sighted. They could see the consequences of what Putin was doing better than the theorists of hybrid war could.

'You'll have to stop him, you know,' the leader of this particular group, his handsome face lined with fatigue, told me one evening. 'If you don't stop him here, you'll have to stop him somewhere else.'

I suppose I agreed, but then didn't the Crimean Russians have a point too? Their enthusiasm to join Russia, with its higher pensions, its certainties, its Soviet nostalgia – all things they craved – was unfeigned, even though their referendum turned out to be a farce. Russian enthusiasm bubbled up everywhere. A couple of days later, I sat on a local bus looking at Twitter, when I read that Putin had signed his decree accepting Crimea into Russia. I couldn't hide my gasp of surprise, and the driver asked me what was up.

'Nothing,' I said. 'It's just that Putin has accepted Crimea into Russia.' He stopped the bus, made me stand up, and instructed me to read the decree out loud. I stumbled over some of the words: bureaucratic language in small letters on my phone's grubby screen. But my audience was rapt. When I finished, my fellow passengers cheered, hugged me and shook my hand, mistakenly believing I shared their delight. Some of them were crying. I tried to smile along but I dreaded what was to come; the rupture that would divide the two halves of my life. There was no way Russia and the West would remain friends after this. The locals here called this the Russian Spring, making a parallel with what had happened in the Middle East. Considering developments in the Middle East, it did not strike me as a happy association.

On the evening of the day of the referendum, thousands of Russians gathered around the statue of Lenin in central Simferopol, where Sergei Aksyonov – a marginal politician and ex-gangster just a month before, now the leader of the peninsula – stood before them in a shiny suit, arms held slightly away from his side. Lasers projected words onto the buildings – RUSSIA, CRIMEA, SPRING – and the crowd chanted along. Loudspeakers boomed out the national anthem, and everyone sang. The music had originally been written for Stalin, but the words had since been changed. I tried to work out which version they were singing, Stalin's or Putin's, but I only know one line – 'Be glorious, our free fatherland' – and that has always stayed the same. It didn't really matter, anyway.

The swelling crowd was feverish, euphoric. The city's emotional circuit was overloaded and there were no breakers to subdue the current. Young men and women drank beer and vodka, and went around Lenin's back for a piss until yellow rivers ran across the marble and off the plinth, saturating the grassy verges. I went back to my single bed at the Sportivnaya Hotel, but I'm not sure anyone else slept. The next morning, a Monday, could have been a hangover, a time of regret, but the party went on. It was incongruous, considering the uncertainty hanging over everything. People queuing to withdraw their savings all but glowed with happiness. They had all voted for Russia in the referendum, and I asked them what they thought would happen to their bank accounts now. Would the currency be changed? If so, at what rate and on what terms? They looked at me like I was insane: none of them had given it any thought. Everything would be fine. Take my life savings, Comrade Putin, and do with them what thou wilt.

I'd been in three countries in just as many days: Ukraine, independent Crimea and Russia, all without moving out of my hotel. I was exhausted. Everyone was exhausted. I decided to leave, to go home, away from the euphoria. At the airport, a woman asked the steward behind the registration desk if our flight to Moscow was domestic or international. 'We are still working on that,' the man answered.

Three border guards, the Ukrainian trident on their sleeves, sat in their cubicles checking passports. They refused to say whom they were working for, or who was paying them, or even what country we were in. The airport's departure board listed flights to Istanbul and Kiev, all marked CANCELLED. Seven months later, even the pretence of alternative destinations would be gone. The airport, like all of Crimea, looked to one place only: Moscow.

5. Bakhchiserai, October 2014

The flight that brought me back to Crimea arrived late in the evening. The airport has no luggage belt, so we waited in the dark for our bags to be loaded onto some shelves under a corrugated roof. Most of my fellow passengers were Russian officials, judging by their suits and their expensive watches, presumably sent down to bring the administration into line. They made me nervous. I had no press card or official permission to be here. Last time, this had been part of Ukraine and I hadn't needed one. Indeed, last time, I'd used Ukrainian hryvnas; now I'd need roubles. My Ukrainian mobile didn't work either, and, like everyone else, I'd need a Russian number. That meant my contact list was worthless: the numbers in it no longer worked. I had no idea how to find anyone, and if I did find someone, they wouldn't be able to find anyone else.

I chatted to a middle-aged woman with hennaed hair and gold teeth, waiting next to me. She had a kind, grandmotherly face, and was called Lilya, a Tatar name, and meeting her relaxed me. She wasn't going to give me a lecture about the West's nefarious foreign policy at any rate, though she did give me a hard time about sitting on the kerb. I'd freeze my bottom, she said, yanking me up by the arm. We talked until our luggage turned up, and then her husband gave me a lift into town. They wondered if they should leave this place. They had a son in London; perhaps they should join him.

In the town of Bakhchiserai, the ancient capital of the Tatars, I went to see Mustafa Jemilev's wife, Safinar. I caught the No. 2 from the bus station and wended through town, past the turning to the Palace of the Khans, past a military base I had last seen when Russian troops were blockading it in the spring, past the usual ex-Soviet low-rise sprawl. Then we turned left, upwards, to what many local Russians still call the Hill of Fools.

The hills above Bakhchiserai are tawny, covered in rough grass that barely obscures the sandy soil. It's pasture for goats, if that. The hills roll gently into the distance, in graceful lines that belie how vicious the winds can be in wintertime, and how cold it can be on the heights.

In the late 1980s, one of these abandoned hilltops began to change, became one of the centres of 'self-return': the Tatars marked out plots, portioned out land and gave each other tasks. To the people living at the bottom of the hill, shaded by trees, they looked insane, toiling away, exposed to the sun in summer, the wind in winter and the rain in spring and autumn. That was when the place got its name: the Hill of Fools.

Most of the Hill is a grid of roughly surfaced roads marking off square plots, each with its own house. The houses tend to be two or three storeys high, each one home to an extended family. Most are still being built – 'A house is never finished,' one local man told me – and some have only just got started. To the right of the road was a plot with a caravan and a toilet on it.

The Hill has two centrepieces. One is Mustafa Jemilev's house, which is large and green and handsome, with the Tatar national symbol etched into the gable end. The other is a mosque, which the community started building in 1993, before most people even had houses. I had visited on a religious festival, and the Tatars had erected a marquee next to the mosque, where old dudes sat on benches, watching their great-grandchildren and muttering in Tatar, no doubt expressing the reservations that the old have about the young all over the world. The wind tossed up dust, and the sun was dazzling. Some men wore skullcaps; others wore Lenin caps. A band of men wearing sparkly suits pumped out swirling Balkan-tinged music, full of brass and passion.

A local official, a recent appointee from the new Russian administration, arrived in a car with a ram in the boot. His assistants hauled it out and handed it to the Tatars as a gift for their festival. The official stood like a boxer, clenching and unclenching his fists, his short dark hair brushed straight onto his forehead, his collar unbuttoned under a charcoal suit, his shoulders squared, as the Tatars thanked him formally on the steps of the mosque. Someone took the ram away, into a plantation of young walnuts. He bucked and jibbed, perhaps aware of what was about to happen. One man held him down while another cut his throat. We watched the scarlet blood pump out, soaking into the grass and the sand. The ram struggled, making two final kicks a full minute after the last blood had trickled out of the great dark open gash in his neck. His eyes were turned upwards all the while, fixing his executioner in his gaze. A woman standing next to me said, apropos of nothing, 'I don't know how anyone could do that to a human being.'

An American radio journalist had turned up with a microphone, and asked the ram-bearing local official if he would stay and help the Tatars eat the mutton. 'I will if I'm invited,' he said, with a tense smile. He didn't stay, and neither did the American.

Safinar, Jemilev's wife, lives five minutes' walk away. She had the forceful manner of female dissidents I had met in Moscow, and it felt incongruous to meet her here, on a hillside overlooking the ancient palace. She made tea and coffee in the hospitable manner of the Tatars, and laid out cakes and sweets.

She and Jemilev moved here in 1989, after a final court case ended with a non-custodial sentence. They had been married for less than a decade, having met when she travelled to Siberia to visit the famous dissident, temporarily in exile between prison stints. When they came to Crimea, her parents had found a little house in the old town with two small bedrooms, and they had all lived there together.

'There were lots of us. My sister and her child, my grandmother, my mother and father, my children, Mustafa and me,' she said, smiling. 'And an uncountable number of guests. Everyone kept coming. Film-makers, journalists, correspondents. If you hadn't been to Mustafa Jemilev's house, you hadn't seen Crimea.'

The house became a de facto presidential palace, if a cramped one – a role that it only lost when this newer and more spacious three-storey building was finished. Jemilev's office is upstairs, but it is empty now. Under the eaves is a sort of museum, a hoard of presents and awards that Jemilev has received in dozens of countries, along with teetering piles of yellowing newsprint: an archive of newspapers detailing the Tatar struggle. On a shelf is the most precious object: a black-and-chrome Panasonic radio given as a gift by Andrei Sakharov when Jemilev halted a hunger strike in the 1970s. There are few allies for the Tatar cause left in Moscow now.

'Look, the Ukrainians suffered as much from Yanukovich and his people as we did; the whole country was looted. They looted so much that Putin could just come in and take this place with his bare hands. But at least under Yanukovich you could take to the streets, protest, make your demands, we could shout about how they were breaking the law. At least they didn't lock us up, arrest us, kill us,' Safinar said.

6. Sudak, October 2014

Travelling by *marshrutka*, or minibus, is by far the easiest way to get around the countries of the former Soviet Union. Minibuses are quick and cheap, and relatively comfortable. I almost never regret choosing a minibus over the regular bus, but this was one of those occasions. I was going from Simferopol to the seaside resort of Sudak, where I planned to stay the night before visiting Jemilev's ancestral village of Ay-Serez. The minibus would take me most of the way and drop me in the village of Grushevka before continuing on the ferry to Russia at Kerch. I sat in the front, between the driver, a heavyset man with stubbled jowls, who remained silent for the entire journey, and a fellow passenger with a strong smell of hangover, who did not.

I speak Russian well enough to baffle most Russians. They normally can tell I'm not Russian, but they tend to think I'm a Slav of some kind: a Serb, perhaps, or a Slovakian. It's rare, anyway, that they'll realise straight away that I'm a Westerner. This man, however, had no trouble. In fact, his insight, considering how unwell he looked, was remarkable. He guessed that I was British before we had even pulled out of the bus station, and that I was a journalist seconds later. He lectured me about both shortcomings for the rest of the journey.

He began, of course, with the fascists. The Ukrainians are fascists, their revolution was fascist, their government is fascist. What were America and Britain doing supporting fascists? What had happened to the solidarity of World War II? Had our grandfathers fought and died in vain? Well, had they?

There were many ways to answer this. In fact, there were too many ways. Where could I even start? I thought for a few seconds, and had a go.

'If the Ukrainian government is fascist, why is the prime minister a Jew?'

Fascists are anti-Semitic; therefore they wouldn't appoint a Jew to head their government: the end. Almost anywhere else, this would have been a fail-safe way to win the argument. Sadly, however, this was one of the places where it wasn't, since it relied on a series of assumptions that were irrelevant to my interlocutor.

To understand where I had gone wrong, you need to know that, in Russian, the word 'fascist' has even less meaning than it does in English. In fact, the Russian word for 'fascist' is probably most accurately translated as 'bastard' or, perhaps, 'foreign bastard'. To Russians, fascists certainly don't need any of the qualities that are part of the mid-twentieth-century movements that share their name, such as anti-Semitism, and are often condemned in language distinctly reminiscent of that once used by fascists themselves.

'Of course he's a Jew, they're all Jews,' the man said.

'What's wrong with him being a Jew?' I asked.

'It means he hates Russians, all Jews hate Russians,' my interlocutor replied.

When I attempted to address some of this convoluted logic, he accused me – and, by extension, all journalists, whom he referred to as 'political prostitutes' – of having poisoned the minds of the world with our lies. He added spitefully that he did not read the Western press any more on principle, to avoid contamination. I wondered which news sources he had previously read.

'Which languages do you know?' I asked, intrigued.

'Russian,' he replied.

'Then, how – ' I began, then gave up gloomfully, aware of the pointlessness of everything.

This more or less went on for the entire journey. Occasionally, I tried to change the subject, to ask him where he was from, or what he was doing here (he was called Vova, hailed from Kostroma, but had lost his home and family a while ago. He now spent his time wandering from job to job. He had come to Crimea to see some friends and was on his way now to see some more, hoping they'd fix him up with work), but these topics never kept him away from fascists for long.

'If Russia hadn't annexed Crimea, what's happening in Eastern Ukraine, the killing, would be happening here. Would you want that?' he asked, just when I thought I'd got him safely onto the topic of his children.

'In the West, you know nothing,' he said, and continued with his litany of complaints about arrogant America, perfidious Britain, Nazi Germany and the whole long list of foreign countries ganging up on Russia.

The landscape rolling past was getting more varied, with conifer-clad hills rising alongside the road, and small houses peeping out above the trees. It was lovely, but I was struggling to concentrate on it. The conversation had made me miserable. A gulf had opened up between Russia and the rest of the world that seemed unbridgeable.

I have spent much of my adult life living in Russia, travelling and exploring, revelling in its endlessly enjoyable language. I love the country. But, sitting in the front seat in this minibus, I felt like I understood nothing. I spoke Russian, sure, but I didn't speak the same Russian as the flock of resentful, strutting bantam cockerels that Putin had hatched into the world.

We pulled into Grushevka, the driver nodding farewell as I moved to get out. My neighbour had to get out too to let me past, stepping down onto the shoulder of the road and waiting while I pulled my bag out from under the seat. He held the door open for me and shook my hand warmly before getting back into his seat.

'It was nice to meet you. Happy travels,' he said, smiling as he pulled the door to. I was left on the side of the road, weary and baffled.

I sat and read for half an hour or so, waiting for another bus. It was a real bus this time, uncomfortable and rickety. My fellow passengers ignored me, and I them. The road sloped up, through conifer groves that would have looked at home in Croatia or the Greek Islands, then snaked downwards: the Black Sea a vague, formless blue splodge in the cleft between the hills. The edges of the day were hazy, and the horizon was a blur, shading into the sky somewhere in the direction of Turkey.

The town of Sudak is a jumble of low-rise buildings overshadowed by the weighty ochre walls of a castle. In the thirteenth century, the Genoese built a colony here to trade with the locals, part of a network of city-state possessions that stretched from the Holy Land, around the Black Sea, to Spain. They are long gone, the castle their only legacy, though Tatars from these parts claim to be lighter-skinned and blonder-haired than their non-maritime compatriots.

Crimea has always been a crossroads, where the silk roads across the steppes met the trade routes of the sea. Goths, Byzantines, Genoese, Jews, Armenians, Bulgarians, Turks, Russians and Ukrainians have all passed through. Each tribe has left a few of its number behind, individuals persuaded to stay by the hills and jagged horizons of the peninsula, by the vines and almond trees.

Until March 2014, Sudak was a popular holiday spot for Ukrainians, who piled into Tatar-owned beachfront hotels. It was an easy train or bus journey here from Kiev, and the seaside and hills were a nice change from the flat steppes of the land to the north.

They weren't here any more, of course. I had most of the town to myself. I had a double room in a little hotel, with two floors of rooms handsomely accessed from balconies around a shared courtyard. Evergreen trees reached up to the light, and fish cruised aimlessly in a pond that looked like it should have had a fountain jetting out of it. My room had a double bed, a bathroom and a window with a sea view. Theoretically, it was comfortable; but then, theoretically this was still part of Ukraine. My room was bitterly cold, the bed nauseatingly damp and entirely without bedding. I was the first guest the owners had had for months and they appeared to have forgotten how to prepare for one. That night I slept wrapped in the carpet, socks on my hands, wearing my coat and two jumpers.

When I first arrived I had had coffee with my hosts and two friends of theirs. A boy who was at school with their niece had been found hanged in the town of Feodosia – the latest of eighteen young Tatar men to have vanished or died mysteriously since the Russian takeover – and they were nervous about having me there, worried about their safety and mine if it became known that a Westerner was in town.

We sat on benches around a low table. They spent much of the time on their phones, whispering in Tatar, passing on rumours, checking facts. The changeover to the Russian phone network had erased all their contacts, as it had mine. The funeral for the boy would be the next day. They wanted to go, but were struggling to find anyone to talk to about it.

I left them there, and looked for somewhere to have supper. The beach was both stony and sandy, like a building site, and studded with strange little plants. A stall advertised 'fresh fish', but didn't have any. I had a beer. Three young men in singlets were leaning on the wall drinking and looking out to sea. Occasionally they turned round and looked into town. Nothing was going on there either.

7. Ay-Serez, October 2014

Ay-Serez, Jemilev's ancestral village, was once, legend says, on the shoreline. Its residents fished happily in the Black Sea, and traded with their neighbours. Then piracy increased, forcing them into the hills. It is a half-hour drive from Sudak. You won't find it on a map, because since the 1940s it's been called Mezhdureche, which means 'between the streams'. There is only one stream here, and no one is sure why anyone thought the name was appropriate.

Ay-Serez is overshadowed on both sides by soaring crags, dramatically spired like something out of the American West. The houses, surrounded by figs, walnuts and almonds, cling to the sides of the valley, looking down onto a stream bed. It was all rocks and pebbles when I visited, but the tufts of flotsam in the trees' branches proved it could be a roaring torrent when it chose.

A group of local Tatars, all elderly, showed me around. Our path took us up the hill, skirting an old cemetery, and past their neighbours' gardens, where dogs barked frantically from the end of chains. We walked in a crocodile along narrow paths cut into the slope, our progress constantly interrupted by tales of who built each house, who had owned it and who lived there now.

We looped down through the village, past a well marked with the Tatar symbol, which visitors whose ancestors came from here like to drink from. We walked up the stream bed, towards the hills. The truck was parked here, a Soviet-made behemoth, its cab sky blue and its flatbed sunset orange. It took strength to turn the key and find first gear, as did turning the wheel, but eventually we were rumbling, bouncing on the over-sprung seats, along the rough track leading into a ravine.

The ravine is called, in Tatar, Darlik Keshmeshi – 'narrow gorge'. At its entrance is a spring, the kind of limpid, shady, ferny, dappled place that might be considered sacred anywhere in the world. It is so perfectly situated that only the least imaginative passer-by would not consider it a gift from a higher power. Travellers entering or exiting the stony wasteland beyond will inevitably stop here, drink the delicious cool water, rest their legs, soak their tired feet.

The year before, a Tatar sculptor had erected a portico over the spring, carved with a sun and bearing the Tatar name of the gorge. He was an amateur and it had been a labour of love, a way of dignifying this lovely place. It was white and simple, and looked rather fine. Or, rather, it had looked rather fine until someone had taken a chisel to it, erasing the Tatar words almost entirely.

In case anyone was in any doubt that the defilement had been intentional rather than a random act of vandalism, within two months two fresh monuments had been cemented into the cliff face. One carried the figure of a bearded man making the two-fingered Orthodox sign of blessing. The other declared the spring holy to Sergius of Radonezh, a Russian saint. Sergius has no known connection to this spring, or indeed to anywhere in Crimea. He does have a connection to Tatars, however. He was the saint who blessed Dmitry Donskoy, Prince of Moscow, before the Battle of Kulikovo, at which the Muscovites defeated the then-dominant Tatars for the first time. He is one of Russian nationalists' most beloved icons. If this addition to the rock face was a hint, it was hardly a subtle one.

We climbed back into the truck, which Rustem, one of the men, heaved round and drove back to the village. Three men awaited us at the end of the track. They wore camouflage, and never turned their eyes away.

They hadn't been there when we set off. Presumably, someone had called them and reported suspicious activity. We got out of the truck but stayed silent, uncomfortable under their scrutiny. They watched us until we reached the top of the hill, their guns held lightly in both hands, and were still watching us until we were out of sight. Lunch was a sombre affair.

8. Kiev, December 2014

It was a Saturday, and a friend and I had gone to see some drones being flown by a man called Yuri. It was cold, way below zero, and Yuri looked at our clothes with disbelief. I thought I'd dressed warmly, but he had recently returned from the front lines and knew better.

We were close to the edge of Kiev, in what had once been a light industrial region, but was now mainly lock-up garages among rotting, derelict factories. We went to a warehouse, gloomy and cold and lined with metal shelves. The shelves and the tables in the centre of the room were piled high with equipment for Ukraine's army. There were bags full of T-shirts and underwear. There were stoves and shovels, camouflage nets and sleeping bags, guitars, ration boxes, water bottles and helmets. There was cutlery and sacks of socks, piles of uniforms and stacks of coats. Much of it had clearly come from abroad: I saw words in English, Italian, French, Russian, Polish and German.

Everything in the room was a gift, donated for the Ukrainian armed forces by well-wishers worldwide. Yuri was a volunteer, one of the many thousands of Ukrainians trying to make up for the deficiencies of the Ukrainian state, which appeared incapable of running an effective military campaign, clothing its soldiers or even just keeping the country together. He told us to take anything we needed. When we hesitated, he took charge: pulling down coats, long underwear, socks, scarves, hats, gloves, boots, holding them up against us to see if they'd fit.

I felt embarrassed: all this stuff wasn't intended for journalists who hadn't dressed warmly enough. Wouldn't someone be angry if we took it? But the old man guarding the store – grizzled beard and thick glasses – just grinned and urged us on. I came out of that warehouse looking like an insurgent, except for the lack of a gun.

Yuri wore a camouflage two-piece suit. It was padded and hooded, and would have made him near-invisible in a sandstone rockery. He had his two drones in the back of his Ford pickup. He and my friend sat in the front. I sat in the crew seat, idly listening to their talk and watching the suburbs of Kiev slide by: shopping centres, high-rise blocks, low-rise districts of garages and stores, then fields, then forest.

We stopped at last, by a track reaching out into a white expanse and dotted with shrubs. I wandered around, killing time, taking photos and keeping my hands warm. We were on an open plain, lines of conifers a kilometre or so away in every direction. The rough scrub poking up through the snow occasionally rose into small trees. The frost had condensed on their branches and when the sun made one of its rare forays through the clouds, the trees glowed magically.

Yuri's drones were made of polystyrene, shaped like two-metre boomerangs, and had two cameras in their wings. The Ukrainian army was outgunned by the Russians, and reconnaissance was crucial, even from modified hobby aircraft such as these. The drones couldn't be controlled remotely because the Russian electronics warfare kit was so sophisticated it would hijack anything that was sent up. Instead, the drones needed a pre-programmed flight path. Yuri was typing coordinates into his tablet computer before getting out of the Ford.

When he had finished, he opened the door, stepped into the snow and picked up a drone. He took it about ten metres away and switched on its cameras. He then held it in both hands so it was pointing upwards. Its twin propellers whirred in a high-pitched scream, and he rose onto his toes, hurling it backwards over his head so it flew off behind him, first vertically, then horizontally.

The drone skimmed the surface of the plain, its starboard wing tip almost touching the few grass seed heads still sticking through the snow this late in the year. Then it rose, climbing towards the treeline. Something was wrong, however. I'd never seen a drone before but I was pretty sure it wasn't supposed to sound like this one: laboured, the high hum of its motors cutting in and out. Seconds later, it dipped and crashed, about five hundred metres away. The engine stopped, and the silence of the forest returned.

We looked at each other. Yuri breathed in through his teeth, and picked up his tablet, hoping it would show him the drone's position. It didn't, so he started to fiddle with it. My friend and I set out without him. The search looked likely to be a long one. We were looking for a white-and-grey drone, two metres long, lying somewhere on a white-and-grey plain, two kilometres wide. I was glad of the warm clothes now.

I set off in the direction it had flown, trying to focus on a small birch tree near the crash site. The ground was uneven beneath my feet. I looked down once to check my footing and, when I looked up, I could no longer distinguish my birch tree from any of the others. I stopped in the region that seemed about right. My friend thought the drone had crashed further away and continued onwards, eventually becoming a brown dot in the distance, disconsolately quartering a section of the plain. I focused on a slope running down to a small stream, for no real reason, but I had to focus somewhere.

Time passed. I gave up on my slope, having walked it twice, and started back towards our original launch site, hoping it would help me find the birch tree. I kept checking over my shoulder: Was it that tree? Or that one over there? One birch tree is much like another when seen from a distance, however, and even the right birch tree would look wrong if seen from the wrong angle. That one perhaps? I wasn't getting anywhere. We had been looking now for at least an hour. My toes felt like small, cold animals: I wriggled them to keep the blood flowing.

Then I heard a small noise. It was a whirring sound, coming from up ahead. I followed it, holding my breath. It stopped, then started again, and I crept closer. At last, there was the drone, flipped over on its back, half buried, its ailerons adjusting as if it were still flying. It had lost one of the stabilising fins on its wing, but otherwise it looked fine. I shouted to the others, waving them over. They looked up, waved back and made their way up the little slope to where I was standing.

'OK,' Yuri said, when he had gathered up the pieces, and we had started back towards the Ford. 'Let's try the second one.' ■

Penobscot Bay, 2013

EPITHALAMIUM

Greg Jackson

Hara had to think there were better ways to say fuck you, although it did take a certain ballsiness, what he had done, in the middle of their divorce no less, and she could see, in fact she couldn't *not* see, that the flip side of this prickishness was the quality she loved in Zeke, loved best in him perhaps, when she did love him, and she did love him – she still did – she just hated him now too. Yes, she would probably laugh about it all when she stopped being so angry. She was always smiling inconveniently in the throes of anger, like the very notion of fury in lives such as theirs dragged a subterranean absurdity up into daylight. But first she would milk her valid rage for the drops of acid in it, the drops with which it had become her job to dissolve Zeke's teasing, so that she could have her part in the cruelty, so that they could pretend they were hurting each other and were equal in this.

Of course she was glad for the company, which made it all a bit awkward. It was rather fun having a companion, another presence to leaven the melancholy of cold gray days. On the hardwood of the living room, beneath lights dimmed to embers, Hara and Lyric moved through their vinyasa poses. The day at that morning hour was often no more than a charcoal disclosure, the small islands rough-hewn ribbons in the fog. On milder afternoons, they kayaked out to the littler islands or explored the rock and shell coves into which the ocean ran. From the beaches they took smooth stones, worn colored glass, and the green and ashen domes of sea urchins, laying them on shelves and window transoms. Lyric did the shopping in town, for which Hara gave her money. When Lyric returned one day with a jigsaw puzzle, they set it up on a painted table looking out to sea, and then in the evenings they would spend an hour or two coaxing forest from piecemeal green, a frame for the puzzle's meadow, so that finally the wolves had something to run across.

Lyric made Hara feel girlish. It had surprised Hara how much she liked the girl. Hara even felt at times that she were the younger of the two, for while it was true what Lyric had said of herself, that she didn't *know* anything, the faultless quality of her spirit made Hara feel petty and irascible and about nine years old. And of course you assumed that what people traded for such easy happiness were lives of ambition and consequence, but it was Hara, wasn't it, who was forty-two, childless, performing a job she liked about as much as washing semen from underwear and getting a divorce?

Maybe Hara had made an error long ago; maybe she had profoundly mistaken the terms of the exchanges she was making. It wasn't envy Lyric brought out in her, no. It was more that Hara had stumbled on a kind of play, as if they were sisters left alone by their parents for the first time to explore the different ways a day could be deconstructed. Hara had never had that with Daeva. The one time she remembered being left under her sister's capricious administration, Daeva had spent the entire weekend shouting at her. Now they lived half a world apart, thankfully, and Daeva hadn't called in close to a year, not since that loony attempt to enlist Hara's help in shipping a metal sculpture to India.

'It's very heavy *and* very fragile,' Daeva had said, as if it took a superior mind to envision such a thing. 'No one who ships that big wants to guarantee it. No one who can guarantee it ships that big. I thought you could do some snooping.'

'Imagine this,' Hara said. 'I'm very busy *and* I don't give a fuck.'

Daeva had proceeded to call Hara a cunt and suggested she wasn't even a very grateful cunt. Grateful for what? Hara wanted to know. For having a sister who had made her tough, presumably, or made her give off the impression of being tough. She didn't ask.

Theirs had never been a family for emotional pleasantries. 'Think of it this way, Hara, darling,' her father had said years ago, at the family home in Haryana after they returned from the States for her final year before college. 'If you let on too readily how you feel, other people will have that over you. They'll know how to make you feel this way or that.' Well, Hara didn't agree – not once she got old enough to have her own opinions and hate her father's she didn't. A lousy servant-class idea, she thought, dressing up powerlessness as strength. But parents' notions got in deeper than you realized and resurfaced when you least expected, least expected to learn you were *like* them, so that you could feel your bleeding heart spilling across the linen tablecloth at dinner only to hear your husband say how *fucking sick* he was of your dignified and embittered reserve. Couldn't you just lose it? Not this stylized sniping anger, but truly undress yourself before him? But if you lived inside me, Hara had wanted to say, you would see I lose it all the time. You make me lose it. You excel at *nothing* so much as making me feel small. And although she didn't say it at the time, she had remarked to herself how strange were the invitations of one's own dignity and restraint, how when you pretended something didn't hurt it only encouraged people to push the blade in deeper.

But so with Lyric: a plausible paradise. The day disassembled into simple tasks, an intimacy that demanded nothing. Hara even felt foolish about how she had reacted on first arriving. Well, it had been startling – a shock – to find someone in the house. And she had come to get away. Two weeks of peace, of distance from the divorce, the endless briefs to compile at work, her martinet trainer and the sympathy dinners, the endless *dinners*, and that new awful flat she was renting in Rose Hill. All up the coast she had felt a current of freedom flowing in from the night, a sweet tidal loneliness indistinct from the damp ocean brine that hung in the air around her as heavy as cloth.

She had made her escape, she thought. So it had been rather a rude surprise to find the cottage occupied – by a stranger, at that, one predominantly naked and perched on a ribbon-like tightrope strung between interior posts.

'Oh, excuse me,' Hara said. 'Who on earth are you?'

The girl dropped to the floor and turned down the soundtrack to some poor toy factory's apparent demolition.

'Sorry?' the girl said.

'No, nothing . . . Just, oh, out of curiosity, what are you doing in my house?'

The girl smiled – as if this were *funny*, as if she were often surprised in panties in the midst of some aerial trespass.

'My parents have this place for the week.'

'Have this place . . .' Hara tested the phrase. 'See, the thing is I own this place, and I'm not in the habit of letting it to the parents of circus performers. Don't tell me they know Zeke.'

'Zeke . . .' The girl shook her head and frowned. 'Something about a charity auction?'

Hara found she was staring at the girl's nipples, tiny shallow cones nearly the color of her skin. She had tattoos running across her body too, garish colorful things that were actually rather pretty. She might have been sixteen or twenty-five. Hara hadn't the slightest idea how old young people were.

'I'd love it if you put a shirt on,' she said.

In the study, waiting for Zeke to pick up, she looked out at the ocean, which in the dark was no more than a suggestive absence, an unbroken pane of black beginning where the dock frame showed in a glimmer of light from the house.

'Zeke, how *are* you?' she said when she heard his voice. 'So, funny thing – you'll like this – there's a girl in my house.'

She heard shuffling on the other end, a word spoken to someone, then Zeke came back on. 'That really could mean almost anything, darling.'

'Don't be a cow, and don't call me darling, you creep. I can hear you smiling over – you know – wherever you are.'

'There's a girl . . . in your house.'

'Zeke.'

'Ah, you mean there's a girl in the cottage, *our* cottage, the one we both own. Well, look, it was whoever won the auction. I didn't know it would be a girl.'

'Oh fuck you that's not the point, you know that's not the point.'

'It was for a good cause, if that helps. Children with rabies or something.'

'You are such an exceptional asshole, do you know?'

'Just think of all the children who won't be running around foaming at their little mouths . . .'

Hara closed her eyes. She wanted to laugh; she wanted to pound Zeke's face until she heard bone crack. It was maddening, just maddening, that since going ahead with the divorce they had been getting on so well, the way they had at first, years before. They went to coffee and sometimes even an early dinner after meeting with the lawyers, like perennial rivals putting a hard-fought match behind them. And that's what it was, a game, a farce. Everything within the ambit of Zeke's restlessness turned into a sort of game. Hara didn't even want his shit, very little of it anyhow. But she did want the cottage, there was that.

'I can see you think this is a riot,' she said, 'but I'd remind you that I'm a lawyer. I have no problem evicting Joan Baez.'

'Joan Baez? Hara, you lost me. But look, there's paperwork, I'll have Cliff send it up tomorrow. And in the meantime you have a new friend, who sounds fun.' But by the time the papers arrived the next day (lupus of all things, Hara knew Zeke did not give two *shits* about lupus) she had decided maybe she liked the sylphlike girl with her absurd name. Maybe she liked having someone around. She always ended up glad for company even when she felt herself most eager to be alone. And Lyric had a serenity about her that was lovely. An irrational part of Hara entertained the notion that Zeke might have done this *for* and not *to* her. Well, it didn't matter. She was happy. The days unfolded along their lazy course. They drank and chatted, read and worked on the puzzle. Lyric showed Hara how to get up on the slackline – that was what you called it. There was no more talk of the charity auction, no talk of plans. Hara checked her impulse to probe the arrangement. Happiness was fragile. You named a happiness to doom it. So she bit her tongue, glancing obliquely just to confirm it was there, still there, and still the next day and the next . . . and so on and perhaps forever, if not for Robert.

The day Lyric returned from town with the news she'd met someone Hara had been busy watching leaves knock about and fall off the trees.

'It was so funny,' Lyric said. 'I asked this guy at the market where I could find something and he didn't hear me. So I said, "Hey, hello, can you understand me?" and he turned around real casually and just goes, "Probably not." Isn't that funny?'

'Funny . . .' Hara said experimentally.

'Oh, and I invited him for dinner. I hope that's all right.'

What could Hara say? *No*? She leaned back in her chair and watched Lyric carry the groceries to the house. 'Crazy girl,' she murmured, feeling just a pang of envy for the girl's ease, her way of making herself at home wherever she was. What had granted her that capacity? Lyric put it down to her childhood: a father who had left her and her siblings to the care of her erratic mother, a woman prone to stints on communes, spur-of-the-moment trips to Puerto Vallarta; life among the whole pack of them, Lyric and her wild brothers and sisters who now, to hear her tell it, pursued vagrancy and addiction, toured with cult-like bands. Her brother Samson, Lyric explained with her natural insouciance, had been kicked out of prep school for murdering his housemaster's dog.

'Murdering?' Hara said.

'Well, they couldn't prove it,' Lyric said. 'But yeah.'

What a funny thing, talking to this girl! Hara worked a puzzle piece into the border and a tree, given a trunk, came to life. She supposed every life could be told as outlandish trivia, decontextualized for the sake of wonder, but it all felt more fanciful from Lyric's mouth, as though, for the girl's very ingenuousness, the treasures of strange accident she blithely enumerated could only flash in the light of your own astonishment.

Well, Hara had her stories too, maybe less incredible than Lyric's, but she could tell them how she liked. In the kayaks paddling out to the islands Hara told Lyric how when she and Zeke camped there, summers, they played a game they called 'sex tag', stripping to boots and chasing each other across the rocky, forested terrain. She felt aroused just recalling it, the peculiar sexiness of nudity above boots, Zeke's cock flopping about as he ran, like a bodily afterthought; how, caught, she might feel the soft rough birch bark against her cheek, holding the tree to steady herself, or how she might squat over Zeke in the moss and feel the floral life of the air everywhere on her body. And then naked and lit in the alpenglow of fucking, as they waved to passing sailboats from the rock beach, how sure Hara had been that of the lives of women and men hers was among the free.

But anything could be a prison it turned out, perhaps most of all the notion that you were free. And once you started to believe in the *idea* of your life, well, the filaments of a cage had already begun to lattice themselves about you, hadn't they?

'But what do you believe?' she asked Lyric.

Their kayaks were close, and Lyric dipped her oar gently in the water as the brightening day carried skeins of mist up from the ocean.

'Hmm,' Lyric said. 'What do I believe about what?'

'Do you see your life as a project?'

Lyric laughed. 'God, wouldn't I be in trouble if I did.'

'But then what is it?' Hara persisted. 'Atomic chaos?'

Lyric shrugged. 'I don't know. This.' She gestured with her paddle.

The water was vitreous before them in the stillness, as though setting into a pale solid – nacre, white opal, shell. At the island they pulled their kayaks onto the pebble beach.

'But you're young,' Hara said. 'It's all right if you don't know yet.'

'You're not so old,' Lyric said.

'Oh, wow. Thanks.'

The mist had cleared under the sun, and the silver sleeve of the ocean ran from fringes of brindled rock to the distant line where it vanished. For an instant it was almost hot.

And Hara was saying Yes, but not all moments were like this, not seizures of glory but the dull poor labor to permit moments of grace, though maybe that was a tired point, wasn't it, and anyway arguing with Lyric was to pretend she had access to some higher knowledge, which clearly she didn't. But Lyric was undressing, Hara saw, her jacket and sweatshirt, her pants, undershirt and bra. She slipped off her underwear and stepped back into her boots, and there she was – not an object of desire so much as of torrential immediacy, shallow nipples, pale skin, fawn ravel above her crotch. The wind caught her hair and blew it as thin as silken wheat. She gave Hara a smirk, her flamelike body, reveled in tattoos, flickering in the wind, and then she was off into the woods.

It was that night Robert came to dinner, arriving promptly, just a few minutes after seven, before Hara even had time to finish her first real drink. He'd brought his dog, Banjo, with him, and a bag of clams.

'Thank you,' Hara said. 'Am I supposed to know what to do with these?'

He gave her a mirthless look Hara had encountered before in this town, the look of boys dead set on being men. He hung up his coat, took the clams back from her and put them in the sink to wash. Lyric had flitted off somewhere, of course – Hara could have strangled her – and now Banjo, after sniffing around the edge for a minute, was attempting to choke down the tasseling on the living-room rug.

'I hate to be a bother, Robert, but I'm sort of fond of that very expensive rug your dog's mauling.'

'Banjo.' Robert spoke sharply to the dog. He had finished rinsing the clams and shook the water from his hands and dried them on a dish towel. 'You've got a nice house.'

'Do you like it? I like it too.'

'I've been here before,' he said. 'Not inside. I helped Gerry clear the yard last spring.'

'You know Gerry then.'

He nodded. 'Lot of downed branches after the storms. We cleared the field and the beech grove you've got.'

'Yes, Gerry said. You did a bang-up job. It looked lovely when I got up this summer.'

Hara saw Robert glance past her and felt Lyric there in his look.

'So you work with Gerry? Look after houses?' she said.

'Some,' Robert said. 'Work where I can. Preston's in the off season.' He pointed his chin at Lyric. 'Where I met this one. Clam some, lobster. Odd repair job. Steamer?' he asked.

'Oh, someplace.' Hara opened the nearest cabinet and closed it. 'My husband was the chef, see. Or when it suited him.'

Robert looked at his palm and rubbed it with his thumb. 'The director,' he said.

'Producer,' Hara said, 'which can only be worse.' She held up a flopping armature she imagined to be a steamer. What pretentious nonsense cooking had become! 'So you're rather a jack of all trades?'

Lyric tongued an olive from its pit in her mouth. 'Robert's in a band,' she said.

'Ah, so odd jobs until you make it as a rock star, is that it?'

'Don't know about that,' Robert said.

'Well, I think it's *perfect*. Lyric here wanders the earth like – like – some sublime nomad, without trade or home, and stumbles on – oh, I don't know – a Yankee handyman or some such. "The vagrant muse and the rooted dreamer." It's like a fable.'

Lyric didn't look up from the joint she was rolling. She licked and sealed the paper and tapped it on the table. Robert rubbed his hands again as the ripe smell stained the air.

Hara finished the vodka nestled among the ice shards in her glass. 'Don't mind me,' she said. 'I'm going through a divorce that has turned me into an absolute monster.'

'One thing for that,' Lyric said. She handed Hara the joint. Hara dragged on it twice before passing it to Robert, thinking how tiresome the courtships of young people were, building in moody pressure until they burst of their own sheer self-importance.

At dinner they were good and stoned. They left the dishes when they were done and took a bottle of whiskey down to the shore. Hara and Zeke had often done this when they had friends up, gathering driftwood for a bonfire at which they sat late into the night, drinking and smoking. The groups were always the same: people Zeke knew from the industry and a few old friends, ostensible adults who because they ate mushrooms once in a while and bore the tattoos of some lapsed rebellion thought they deserved medals of nonconformity or abiding hipness. Well, Hara got it. It was easy to fall into that way of thinking when you were high and tuned in, or so it seemed, to the hidden correspondence that bound your life to the mantling commerce of heaven and earth. Possible, for instance, to see the sparks the driftwood sent up answering a call, passing up and out of sight to cool and settle as the ivory points high above. Possible, if you cared to, to see yourself outlined in their grid.

'So who gets the house?' Robert said.

Hara laughed. 'Robert,' she said, a hand to her chest. 'My!' Not that she minded a little bluntness. 'Oh, who knows. I hope I do. My husband's such a shit.' She took a sip from the bottle and passed it along. 'I feel like some shrill hausfrau complaining, but you know the *distance* you travel – I mean, mentally – it just kind of shocks you.' She looked at the sea, aglow beneath the moon. 'You spend so long assuming it will all just fall into place – successful, doting husband, kids, the whole *tableau* – and when it doesn't, you start to compromise – a little here, a little there – and slowly, bit by bit, any sense you had of what was supposed to happen falls away, just slides off into the ocean, until there you are, alone, on a little island called your life.'

They stared at the fire for a minute, then Robert knocked his head back toward the cottage. 'Not the worst island.'

Right, Hara was spoiled, dreadfully spoiled, although it didn't make a bit of difference.

'It's like the frog,' Lyric said. 'You know, put it in boiling water and it jumps out. But heat the water *ever so slowly . . .*'

'Yes, people are always saying that, but how do they really know?' Hara said. 'Who has all these frogs and pots and no lids and, like, this pressing need to boil frogs alive?'

'I've known some people,' Robert said.

'Perhaps you have met my husband,' Hara said.

Banjo barked then to be petted, and Hara saw Robert catch Lyric's eye. She should leave them, she knew, that was the decent thing to do. Only she didn't want to. She didn't want to go to bed and wake up and have it be tomorrow and then the next day. She didn't want to go inside and be alone. If she ever had to be alone again it seemed she might disembowel herself with a skill saw. When had she become like this? Or, that was euphemistic, wasn't it – the question was, when had she *become* this? It would be very easy to blame Zeke or the divorce, but hers was a condition, was it not? This desperate need for people, all of whom she loathed. Even the ones she liked she loathed – and that was the maddening thing about people. If you grew remotely fond of them you were timid and resentful, waiting for them to pull away; and if you didn't they grew tiresome at the speed of light. She had her college friends, a few, and her law-school friends, four or five women spread around the country and globe, busy with their jobs and children, and yes, they could speak to one another like sentient creatures and every so often wash up together for an hour on the shores of lucidity. But only a lunatic would call that *companionship*. Or the fifty-minute phone sessions with her therapist, because Lord knows she was too busy to physically go see him, and drinks with colleagues that ended at 6.45 after chattering on with the absentmindedness of watering a garden, waiting your turn to offer some idiotic little discourse on the numbing fiction that was your public life. *Marc and I just started kite-surfing. Oh, you don't say. We picked it up in Mauritius over the holidays. How remarkable*

– I can't think of a single thing I give less of a fuck about. And then Zeke or the equivalent threading some conversational déjà vu with that rote inattentive teasing, his mind clearly elsewhere, until you managed to get upset enough to exact maybe twenty minutes' careful listening to expressions of *how things make you feel* and apologies roughly as nourishing as swine flu, and those twenty minutes it turned out, for a surprisingly long time, were just enough to build back the hollowed little Jenga tower of your collapsing marriage.

No thank you, really. Hara would do without if it came to that. She was proud enough to prefer suffering to fooling herself, which was only a less dignified form of suffering. Only why were they all so *busy*, she and Zeke and her friends? What were they rushing around for when they could have been gazing at each other over pretty dinners, talking aimlessly of Life, of what exactly they were doing on this earth? Was it really just a matter of appearances, that tired game of posing your life next to other people's to see which was a little more special, a little more or less grand in the scheme of human savagery? All that anecdotal one-upsmanship, who you knew, and sending your kids to fucking Trinity? If you *had* kids. Yes, it was those things, but it couldn't only be. Wasn't it also the great yawning nothing beneath? You could be lonely in the middle of ten million people or lonely all by yourself, but the two *felt* different.

The phone rang in the house. Hara heard it rise shrilly above the quiet. Zeke again. She'd been ignoring his calls, but now she needed to excuse herself anyway.

'All right, you've got me,' she said. 'What do you want?'

There was a pause. 'Is Boris, I call from Russia.'

'Zeke.'

'Boris,' Zeke said. 'Anyway, there you are. I left you a hundred messages.'

'That sounds off by a zero or two.' Hara picked up a framed picture from the desk as she spoke: she and Zeke at a wedding on Skiathos. They looked – well, formidable. 'In any case, I thought not answering was my own sort of message.'

'You're not back in New York then.'

'Oh my God, what a master sleuth you've become!'

'Hara.'

'Are you having me followed? Is there a man with binoculars in the hedges?'

'Look, I wanted to see how you are. Make sure you weren't hacked to bits by your house guest or whatever.' When Hara didn't respond, he said, 'Anyway, she must be gone by now.'

'Nope,' Hara said.

'Really.'

Oh, how she hated that crystallizing attention in Zeke's voice, the colossal distraction it laid bare!

'It's been more than a week,' Zeke said.

'Yes, I'm able to count,' said Hara. 'You were right, actually. I made a new friend. She's fun.'

'You sound odd, Hara.'

'Well, I'm drunk. And stoned. And if you must know I'm hosting *two* young people tonight, and I need to get off the phone with you in a minute so we can all go make love in front of the fireplace.'

'Hara.'

'Hmm? Or does that sound like you, Zeke? Now really, don't you have some cardboard Tanya to escort around Bel Air or what are we talking about?'

She could feel him pinch the bridge of his nose. It was strange to be talking just like this, two specks in a mind-numbing enormity, alive in each other's ears. The night seemed for an instant too big for thought to encompass, blackness billowing from the cottage to envelop the cities of the world – the numberless small huddlings of light, people, rooms, countless tiny rooms, in one of which, somewhere, was Zeke – seeping out from those pinpoints of light, this blackness, to fill all the unfathomable elsewheres, the vast empty tracts, forests and ice fields, enormous lakes torn into the wilderness, plains splayed with winds wreathed in unanswered howls.

'I don't know when you're being serious anymore,' Zeke said.

'That's funny,' said Hara, 'because now I'm racking my brain for when you were *ever* serious.'

'I'm worried about you. Should I be worried?'

'The thing is' – her voice had fallen, the spite deserting her that quickly – 'you don't have to be worried about me anymore. More to the point, I'm not sure you *get* to be. Hanging up now.'

He let her. She lay on the window seat and closed her eyes, careering for a minute on the tide of intoxication that bore her. She was drunker than she had realized, good and stewed, but what good was *that* when no one would rise to her bait? Why were people so horribly decent only just after they had knifed you in the Theatre of Pompey? I come to praise Hara, not to marry her! And what had she been thinking, really, when Zeke *had* come to marry her? Well, it wasn't hard to remember, just hard now to account for the feeling of possibility that had crept in to scatter her prudent doubts. It had been a beautiful wind-bitten day in the hills above Sorrento, sharp and bright, with thin, high clouds trailing out as far as the eye could see. The cool air startled the night's muzzy vestige, a night when they had drunk too much and stayed up talking and making love. And how Hara loved that feeling of days that propelled you for their very clarity into an unarmored sense of your own vital heart. She had known what was coming. She knew from how few calls Zeke had been taking. And then what he said had been more like a little argument, really, a comic's monologue. *Hara, look, I'm getting on, you know, long in the tooth and all that, and you're – well, you're young, but you might want kids one of these days. And I have this ring, I thought it would look pretty on you. But it's the kind of ring where if you put it on, you know, it means more than just, Now I'm a person wearing a ring. It means – fuck – I don't know, 'I've entered into a celestial partnership,' something horribly sentimental like that . . .*

'Oh, for fuck's sake,' Hara finally had to say, but she was laughing. And beneath her hesitance, her judicious dread, her sense that in even his sweetest moments Zeke was watching himself and not her, beneath it all her heart beat hollow little yeses. It made her want to throw up, it did *now*, for even if the reasonableness of her objections would be borne out – that Zeke was not a person who came to rest and perhaps neither was she – all she could think just then was that it was happening to her, the thing you wait for, telling yourself you aren't waiting, sure someday it will come, and sure just the same it won't, that you will be the one passed over while the insufferable millions walk hand in hand into the insipid lava of a setting sun. But Hara would be one of them, she saw. She felt the dull embrace of that contentment enfold her like curtains from the wings. She took the ring Zeke gave her and held it to the sky. Inside, the sky looked like Earth seen from space, a vast tiny sky as big as the bigger sky all around. And as she adjusted to its weight over the next few days, she marveled that without this anchor, for so many years, she hadn't floated up, up and out of sight, to the point far above where the things you could once see right in front of you disappear.

When Hara awoke, it was morning. A gray sky lingered just above the treetops, and around her was a blanket she didn't recall getting. Lyric was in the living room reading when she emerged from the study.

'Morning. We thought we'd let you sleep.'

'Oh. Is Robert – '

'No, but he says thanks.'

Hara doubted that very much. The room was neat, though. The remains of a fire lay in the fireplace.

'He seems nice,' she said, lying down on the couch. Lyric rose to fill two glasses of water. 'Maybe a little surly, the strong silent type, I suppose, but to each her own.'

They worked on the puzzle that afternoon. Their progress was slow but undeniable. The field had begun to form in swatches of emerald cloud, floating within the forest. The wolves galloped at the center, shabby specters seeking purchase. Hara wondered if wolves really ran like that, in large packs through open fields. We spoke of wolf packs and lone wolves – but which was it? Did we have our symbolism straight?

The grim weather held. Their routine held too, mostly, though in its repetitions and departures Hara sensed a strain. Maybe it was no more than Lyric's taking the car at night to visit Robert, or that when Hara pressed her for girlish confidences she grew defensive and vague. 'We're just friends,' she said.

'Right, and I'm friends with vodka,' said Hara. Then Lyric would sigh and say Hara didn't understand, that she was done with love and romance. It was too much trouble.

'You're twenty,' Hara said.

Too much trouble? Who didn't want trouble?

She phoned the firm to tell them she was staying on, fire her if they liked. 'Don't be dramatic,' said her boss. When Lyric left her in the evenings, Hara pulled down Zeke's pretty cookbooks, gazing at the pornographic dishes before settling on another dinner of cheese and crackers paired with a bottle or two of expensive wine. Sometimes she removed pieces from the puzzle, only a few here and there. When she couldn't focus enough to read, she went through the shoeboxes of family photos, the unsorted record of her childhood, the years in India and Britain and those vile teenage years in DC. She liked their family vacations best, trips to balmy coasts, where the bars along the shore glowed in strings of colored lights and tiny waves lapped at the beach. After her parents went to bed, with Daeva holed up in their bedroom calling some boy, Hara often wandered the beachfront alone. There was nothing for her, she was too young, but the music from the bars sounded to her like the harsh mystery of adult happiness. And as she drifted in the furling breeze, straining to hear into the places she was not allowed, a part of her tended the implausible hope that someone would know to come out and lead her inside, not to one of the bars, not to any one room, but to the secret chamber of possibility where real life took place.

On the nights Lyric stayed in things were better. If Hara were feeling bold she would ask to see Lyric's tattoos. She knew them by now, the sinewy thicket, on the girl's shoulder, of green tangles bursting here and there in a red corolla, the ox-eyed nymph washing fruit in a brook. The brook flowed beneath the flowers, ran out into a river and a shimmering ocean that crossed Lyric's back and washed up below a fishing village, an outpost of sand and stilted huts. Above the village a city rose into the ochre sky, sunlight spilling onto the clouds where a pair of naked angels embraced and an Amazon warrior, with one breast and a sword, sat on a throne. Then on the girl's neck, errant rays of sunshine fed a painted vasculature, turned from gold to red, merging back into the flowers and carrying the crimson blood along green stems to the calyces where the roses bloomed.

Sometimes it seemed to Hara that if she looked hard enough she might find herself there, a timeless fixture in the fretwork prophecy, and that if she did it might settle certain nagging questions. Other times she thought, *Enough of that.* The new moon, which at first greeted her as an absence, had gone full term and now was emptying. Flakes of snow fell on the ocean and dissolved softly into it. Maybe I can live here, she thought, and dissolve into the ocean myself, into the islands and forests, with their thickets of bitter harshness. Maybe Robert will die, or grow uninterested, or cruel. Maybe Lyric and I will go live on an island like half-wild beasts.

'What if you stayed on?' she said to Lyric one day. 'When I go back, I mean. You could keep an eye on the house for me.' When Lyric didn't say anything, she added, 'I'd pay you, of course. Well, think about it.'

Another time she said, 'You feel like real life is going on someplace else. You're young. You think if you keep searching you'll find the place you're meant to be.'

'I don't think that,' Lyric said. 'I've been to Morocco.'

Sometimes Hara wished Lyric *would* leave. Because the girl's presence had become the augury of its absence, it often seemed the worse of the two. It was no longer pleasure Hara felt in her company but the compulsion to ensnare something elusive, something fleeting – the urge to establish a state of permanence, if not of happiness, one able to withstand her endless attempts to tear it down.

On the night of the party they stayed in drinking joylessly, and Hara asked Lyric whether she'd given it any more thought.

'Given what more thought?' Lyric said.

'The Church's views on women. What do you think? About staying on.'

Lyric seemed to be *pouting*, if such a thing were possible. Hara wondered if imploring her to stay home had been such a good idea. The party sounded ghastly though. The idea of hearing Robert's band play made Hara expectantly ill.

'You'd be near Robert,' she went on. 'I'd be up more often . . .'

Lyric had taken a piece of decorative fruit from the wooden bowl, a papier-mâché pomegranate, and now was rolling it across the table. When Hara didn't say anything more, she stopped.

'What is this fixation with Robert?' she said. 'Why does it matter? Anyway, I've told you, we're *friends*.'

'All right, God,' Hara said. 'Did you ever hear about the lady who protested too much? But let's go to the party if it's going to be like this.'

'A minute ago you didn't want to.' Lyric looked morosely at her glass. 'You said someone named Dwayne was going to sneeze Type 2 herpes in your cornea.'

'I don't think I said that. Anyway, I can't be responsible for every dreadful remark that escapes my mouth. Don't you want to go?'

'It's late.'

'Oh, it's barely ten. I bet there's still some chip detritus to be had, or whatever they eat.'

'*They*?'

'I'm *joking*. The Morlocks.'

They left, finally, after arguing about a dress. In fairness Lyric had warned Hara that the party would be outside, although Hara had only half believed her. It was next to a building site, a new house going up. There was a fire, at least, and a slight rippling heat from the crowd dancing – if that was the word – before the plywood platform where a few underdressed young men were in the process of trying to damage some instruments. Hara shivered and pulled her jacket around her.

'I told you,' Lyric said.

'You don't have to gloat.' Hara took a shot of bourbon, then filled her plastic cup. 'What?' she said to Lyric. 'Oh God, we're not going to have that kind of evening, are we?'

She moved away to establish a little sphere of independence and in the thick sweet odor of the fire caught a second scent, bodily and intimate. She saw a man with a small pipe pressed to his lips.

'Excuse me,' she said. 'Hi, would it be a terrible bother . . . ?'

'Be my guest,' the man said through a held breath.

He was likely a few years older than Hara, or at least his face had seen a lot more sun. She took the pipe from him and sucked the flame over the embers while he gazed off at the stage.

'Shit that passes for music these days.' He shook his head.

'They said the same about Schoenberg, though, didn't they?' said Hara.

What on earth was she talking about? How old did this man think she *was*? She was, she realized, exactly the age Zeke had been when they married. She tried to hold the thought still, to explore it for deeper meaning, but her attention was deserting her. The lights around her, blazing at points along their catenaries, edged into a sharper dazzle.

'Don't believe I know you,' the man said.

'No, it's unlikely,' Hara agreed, taking his hand. It felt like clay in her smaller, softer hand, the hand of a golem. 'Where, um – do we pee in the bushes then?'

He laughed. 'Probably your best bet. There's a porta-potty down the road, but plumbing won't go in for another month or two.'

'Oh, is it your house?' Of course it wasn't – what was she thinking?

'No, no. House like this?' He laughed. 'Summer folk, you know. All the new construction, really.'

'Do you feel invaded then, is that it?'

'Ha,' the man said, looking at her for what she felt was the first time.

Yes, of course, she was hated. They all were, seasonal invaders, self-important snobs from their effete enclaves bringing the entire economy with them but full of prissy needs and ideas – their impossible diets, their fussy attachments to foreign wine and East Asian calisthenics. So particular and helpless, weren't they, babes in the woods when it came to anything practical, but not above affecting a chummy tone and shedding grammar to mingle with the brutes who cleared their lawns and fixed their toilets. Well, Hara would love to see them try the contract law on a corporate merger. Or, no – what she did was stupid too. But the *dissonance*. How did anyone manage to go anywhere or talk to anybody? Oh, but wasn't she grateful for her privilege and opportunities? Oh, yes, she was *awfully* lucky. And weren't the people who built things and fixed toilets just *awfully* dignified? Oh, yes – they *were*. Oh, hooray! Hooray for all of us! Hara tripped over a root and righted herself, just.

'Easy there,' Lyric said. 'Are you OK?'

'I am, thank you,' Hara said. 'And I don't need to be babysat.'

Lyric was silent.

And how Hara loathed her! All of it – her simplicity and openness, the opacity of her openness, the light flitting quality of her affection, her quiet restraint.

'You think it's so easy,' she said, 'traipsing around, without a plan or care in the world, without a job or money – but not to worry! Throw yourself on the mercy of fate! How magical life is – fa la la!'

Lyric pushed a twig with the toe of her shoe. 'I never said it was easy.'

'No. But you don't buy the groceries, do you? Or the gas for the car that takes you to and from what's-his-name's house? Or the heat that keeps us from freezing? Or the electricity, etc., etc.?'

'So?' Lyric said. She said it as an actual question and so simply that Hara lost her point. What was her point? Something stupid, clearly.

'Right. *So*. So what? So *what*? Let's just wear flannel and mosh to Nirvana and say "So what?" when life gets, like, totally annoying.'

Lyric laughed. 'What are you talking about?'

'I don't know,' Hara said. 'I don't know, and now I have to pee. So excuse me.'

She pushed past Lyric down a path in the woods. When she had finished, she followed the path the rest of the way to the water, to the shoreline strip of dark rocks where a downed white tree shone a ghostly color in the moonlight. She sat and lit a cigarette.

'You missed us play.'

Hara started but didn't turn.

'How'd it go?' she said. She could feel his presence behind her. When he didn't answer, she said, 'I heard a different band play. If you sounded anything like them, never might be too soon.'

He made a brusque sound through his nose, a joyless laugh, and Hara looked up to see him light his own cigarette, face yellowed in the flame.

'Strange thing, you and Lyric,' he said.

'I know,' Hara said. 'What are the chances? My husband's such a twat.'

He dragged on his cigarette and blew out the smoke. 'Wasn't what I meant.'

'Oh, it wasn't? What *did* you mean? Strange that we got along? That I let Lyric stay on and it all worked out?' She looked out at the islands. She should have built the house out there, hidden in the woods – a tree house, with crenellations to fire arrows through. 'You got an all right deal, though, didn't you?'

'What do you want from her?' he said. It thrilled Hara to hear the note of exasperation in his voice.

'Oh, I don't know. What is it *you* want from her? Companionship? Loyalty? A little appreciation? Those sound like places to start.'

'Jesus,' he said.

'Are we fighting, Robert? Are we fighting over Lyric or what exactly? Are you her protector, do you imagine, her knight in armor, come to save her from me?'

He met Hara's eye. She wanted to laugh. Did he think he could *frighten* her? '

'You treat people like – '

'People, Robert, let themselves be treated this way or that way.'

'So what – you use people? You want people to bow down to you?'

'Bow down . . .' Hara shook her head in incomprehension. 'Well, now that you mention it, that *does* sound nice. Or just one person, really. There could be one person, and they would bow down to me, and I would bow down to them. It would be a little arrangement, see? We would both bow down, and then we'd be on the floor so it'd be quite natural to start fucking.'

'People like you . . .' Robert flicked his cigarette away.

'People like me,' Hara said. 'Go on.'

'It's – ' Oh, he did seem childish, struggling to find his words. 'You can't just – sometimes you have to be *invited*,' he said. 'You are or you aren't. It isn't up to you.'

Hara laughed and clapped her hands together. 'Oh, bravo, Robert! *Thank you.* Thanks for letting me know. Only wait till you get older and those invitations dry up . . . But perhaps I owe you quite a lot, is that it? Or does the world owe you something? For your honesty? Or for the clams – how could I forget? For cleaning the yard, there's that, stacking fruit in the market . . .' Hara stood as she spoke, a glorious ringing pressure in her head. She felt a destructive element swim into the night as beautiful and wild as the surf below. 'Or what about for your masculinity? Your rugged good looks, your brooding silence . . . Does it take an awful lot of restraint? And now you have to listen to some spoiled bitch – because that's what I am, right? A spoiled bitch tossing about handfuls of glitter, expecting you to be grateful. But you have to clean the glitter up, don't you? That's your job. Sweeping up all the glitter spoiled bitches leave around.' She could feel him growing smaller as she drew near. Something ugly and uncertain softened his face. He seemed suddenly so insubstantial – what *nothing* he was – flinching when she touched him. Was it possible he knew anything, anything at all, she didn't? Was his resentment anything more than his confusion, his boundless confusion and the sexual terror that boiled in men? It was enough to make her sick. She snorted faintly, feeling how easy it would be to crush him, letting herself down to her knees and saying to herself, Well, OK then, throwing her cigarette to the side and undoing his belt, the button of his jeans. She looked up at him. 'Is this what you wanted, Robert? Is this what bowing down looks like to you?' He stiffened as she took down his pants and underwear. She held him, gathering her hair behind her and taking him in her mouth. It was like taking a small apple into her mouth whole, like cleaning a small apple without breaking the skin. And then it came back to her – what men liked, how easily they were cowed.

She wanted – what she wanted just then – was for Zeke to see her, and her father, their *jewel* defiling herself and for nothing, for no more than the monstrousness of their own vanity. Her, the daughter of a goddamn Indian ambassador, wed so regally and for all to see, front and center in the *Times* notices. Look, Daddy! Look, Zeke! *Look* . . . But even as this wish broke the surface of her mind she knew it couldn't carry her. She felt it fall away and an exhaustion take its place; she was bereft – of even shame and anger – bereft with only her life before her, all the many things that made it up, her job and her few friends, the apartment, the cottage, the knowledge that it would all be there waiting for her tomorrow and the next day and through all the days ahead – days demanding to be filled because even if you got rid of the *stuff* there would still be days. Time had to be filled, one way or another. And what an obligation it was! She would be put away. Yes, she saw it now, consigned to a clean white ward with white walls and TVs and people who told her what to do and what not to do; and Daeva would visit once a year, citing concern but really there to gloat, to take pleasure in her sister's ruination. 'If only you'd been less sure you were special,' she would say. 'Less certain the world *cared*. But you were always very self-involved, weren't you?' And Hara would nod agreeably, stilled in the lovely sedation of pills from small plastic cups, flooded – yes, that's how it would feel – *flooded* with the wondrous indifference of no longer having a life to fight for, an identity to pretend was hers.

She was swimming, out in the weed and booze, in a spiraling consciousness that dizzied her as she pushed into the churning blue.

Her parents were calling to her. 'Hara, not so far!' She could feel the vast mindless power of the waves below her, driving and lifting her, driving and lifting.

She did not remember getting home. When she heard Lyric speak, she felt the project of locating herself in space and time crash in on her with such violence that it seemed she might never pull clear.

'Hey, are you all right?'

Hara was in the living room, her own living room – that seemed true. Yes, on the sofa. She could feel it now as more than a cloud holding her aloft. Was it daytime? It was. Lyric sat facing her, a magazine open on her thigh.

'I think . . . I'm alive,' Hara said. 'You look like a friend of mine, but I know the Devil takes many forms.' She tried to catch Lyric's eye. 'I'm only joking.'

'I'm leaving soon.'

'To town or . . . ?'

Lyric was silent. In the stillness Hara saw something flash at the periphery of her consciousness, something terrible. She squinted. She couldn't quite make it out, flitting and darting among the trees. Another flash. It nearly gave itself up, dodged away, dashed this way and that, almost at hand . . .

Then she saw it.

'Ah,' she said. She hoisted herself up – it took some effort – and went to the kitchen to make coffee.

'And where will you go?' she asked, filling the machine. 'Do you know?'

Lyric shrugged.

Hara shook her head. 'Just friends,' she said under her breath, too softly, she thought, for Lyric to hear.

But Lyric said yes and laughed once. '*Just.*'

It was Robert's car Lyric piled her stuff into. That figured. Hara couldn't see into the driver's seat and she didn't go out. She stood near the doorway with her coffee and watched Lyric carry out her bags.

'Well,' Lyric said when she was done. 'Bye.'

'Bye,' Hara said and felt that crippling dignity hold her in the door frame and seal her lips.

But the things she could have done, the things she could have said!

She watched the car drive away and listened until the sound of its tires on the drive faded. Then she took her coffee to an armchair. She didn't move until the sun began to dip in the sky.

By evening she felt better. She got up and wandered around the house. How big it was! How quiet. Had it always been so big or was it bigger in the silence? The lights were off and shadows lengthened across the room. The early evening was turning golden outside. The light seemed to burn as it fell, catching on the lawn, scattering on the ocean. There was the puzzle. Her hand had fallen on it without her realizing. God, she had been crazy, truly crazy, to think Lyric couldn't leave until it was done. She touched it tenderly for a moment, the stiff-edged cardboard, the soft joints between the pieces. Then on an impulse she swept it to the floor. The sun pulsed. Good riddance, she thought. The sun pushed into the clouds, *good riddance*, pushed through the clouds, and then she saw them, the wolves. Out in the meadow the pack was running. The sun caught on their backs as they tore across the grass. They reminded her just then of the golden jackals she had heard calling from the grasslands in her youth. On the darkening porch she heard the jackals calling and her mother calling – 'Haaaaaaaaa!' – summoning her to another of their prim and stately dinners. She strained for a moment to hear the jackals. She wanted to join them, as if such a thing were possible! They were deniable, she supposed, the wolves. What else? The girl? Well, not everything. The trees around the yard were so much fiber and pith. Milkweed and primrose flowered here in the spring. The moon was rock, Hara thought. The ocean so many particles of water. And people – what did they say? – minerals and proteins, was it? Minerals and proteins who ate to persist. Who slept to persist. Who fucked to persist. At some point the stories had to stop. At some point the wolves died, the people died. The alarm clock went off. The particles did what they did and at times, out of chaos, suggested order. And at times, out of chaos, dashed order. And at times, who knew? The facts were stubborn. They were also stories. Quite a lot, in other words, was left to interpretation. But moments continued to come, this one on the last one's heels. And a new one. And a new one. And a new one.

'Lyric,' Hara nearly called into the empty house. 'Lyric, come look!' ■

Did you know that print subscribers to *Granta* also get access to over one hundred and thirty back issues on granta.com? That means . . .

Diana Athill **Margaret Atwood Iain Banks** Julian Barnes
Ned Beauman Fatima Bhutto Roberto Bolaño
Anne Carson Eleanor Catton **Noam Chomsky**
Bret Easton Ellis **James Ellroy Louise Erdrich**
Jonathan Franzen **Janine di Giovanni**
Nadine Gordimer Mark Haddon Seamus Heaney
A.M. Homes Nick Hornby **Kazuo Ishiguro A.L. Kennedy**
Stephen King **Nicole Krauss Doris Lessing**
Nelson Mandela **Hilary Mantel Ian McEwan**
David Mitchell Lorrie Moore Herta Müller **Alice Munro**
David Peace Mary Ruefle **Salman Rushdie**
Taiye Selasi **Will Self Gary Shteyngart Zadie Smith**
Rebecca Solnit **Andrea Stuart Paul Theroux**
John Updike Binyavanga Wainaina Joy Williams
and Jeanette Winterson

. . . to name a few.

Not a subscriber? Visit granta.com or complete the form overleaf.

GRANTA

THE MAGAZINE OF NEW WRITING

PRINT SUBSCRIPTION REPLY FORM FOR UK, EUROPE
AND REST OF THE WORLD (includes digital access).
For digital-only subscriptions, please visit granta.com/subscriptions.

GUARANTEE: If I am ever dissatisfied with my *Granta* subscription, I will simply notify you, and you will send me a complete refund or credit my credit card, as applicable, for all un-mailed issues.

YOUR DETAILS

TITLE ....

NAME ....

ADDRESS ....

POSTCODE ....

EMAIL ....

☐ Please tick this box if you do not wish to receive special offers from *Granta*
☐ Please tick this box if you do not wish to receive offers from organisations selected by *Granta*

YOUR PAYMENT DETAILS

1) ☐ Pay £32 (saving £20) by Direct Debit

    To pay by Direct Debit please complete the mandate and return to the address shown below.

2) Pay by cheque or credit/debit card. Please complete below:

    1 year subscription: ☐ UK: £36   ☐ Europe: £42   ☐ Rest of World: £46

    3 year subscription: ☐ UK: £99   ☐ Europe: £108   ☐ Rest of World: £126

    I wish to pay by   ☐ CHEQUE   ☐ CREDIT/DEBIT CARD

    Cheque enclosed for £ _____ made payable to *Granta*.

    Please charge £ _____ to my: ☐ Visa ☐ MasterCard ☐ Amex ☐ Switch/Maestro

    Card No. ☐☐☐☐☐☐☐☐☐☐☐☐☐☐☐☐

    Valid from *(if applicable)* ☐☐ / ☐☐   Expiry Date ☐☐ / ☐☐   Issue No. ☐☐

    Security No. ☐☐☐

SIGNATURE .... DATE ....

Instructions to your Bank or Building Society to pay by Direct Debit

BANK NAME ....

BANK ADDRESS ....

POSTCODE ....

ACCOUNT IN THE NAMES(S) OF: ....

SIGNED .... DATE ....

DIRECT Debit

Instructions to your Bank or Building Society: Please pay Granta Publications direct debits from the account detailed on this instruction subject to the safeguards assured by the direct debit guarantee. I understand that this instruction may remain with Granta and, if so, details will be passed electronically to my bank/building society. Banks and building societies may not accept direct debit instructions from some types of account.

Bank/building society account number

☐☐☐☐☐☐☐☐

Sort Code

☐☐☐☐☐☐

Originator's Identification

☐9☐ ☐1☐ ☐3☐ ☐1☐ ☐3☐ ☐3☐

Please mail this order form
with payment instructions to:

Granta Publications
12 Addison Avenue
London, W11 4QR
Or call +44(0)208 955 7011 Or visit
GRANTA.COM/SUBSCRIPTIONS for details

Creative writing
courses and retreats

ARVON

"These are
life-enhancing
weeks"
—Simon Armitage

arvon.org

**Fiction, Poetry, Non-Fiction
& Life Writing, Theatre, Film,
TV, Radio, Writing For Children**

LOTTERY FUNDED

Supported using public funding by
**ARTS COUNCIL
ENGLAND**

© MARTHE JUNG
Plongeon, 2012

THE CAGE OF YOU

Kerry Howley

I do not fear doctors, surgery, medicine or modernity, but in the spring of 2014, this I knew: If you let them, they'd slice you open on their own time. American medical professionals were wild for the surgical removal of term fetuses. Caesarean rates spiked at twelve and four, hours when doctors were nearing the end of their shifts, sleep-heavy and eager to leave. If they couldn't get at the baby direct, if he slid canal-ward before they could carve him out, they'd take a knife to the perineum, outspreading the point of exit so they could more quickly make their own. In every case, they'd go first for a needle to the spine. They wanted you numb. They wanted you docile.

I would give birth in a bath, awake to the pain. My reasons were scientific, my sources peer-reviewed. There would be a quiz later, and I would ace it. I chose a doula based on the selectivity of her college, met with her at a chic cafe where the tables were high and small.

'I want to reduce my child's chances of antibiotic resistance,' I said, and meant, 'Please don't talk about my "birth journey".' 'I do not want the baby to bear the risks of synthetic oxytocin,' I said, and meant, 'Please do not offer to preserve my placenta.'

'That seems very . . . rational,' Katherine said, with care. Katherine was smart. She had been to a very selective college. She slid the contract across our tiny table. There were options, extras, deluxe packages for the naturalest among us. 'Doula Services'. Check. 'Childbirth Education'. Check. 'Delivery of First Placenta Smoothies'. There were second smoothies? No check. I filled in the blanks, signed on the line, slid the contract back.

M y late twenties were spent among a dozen mixed martial artists, cage fighters, 'ultimate fighters' if you like. I was writing a book. They were living their lives. Each fight took months of studied preparation, a kind of refined writhing in an abandoned storefront. They trained in boxing, in wrestling, in ju-jitsu and judo. Sometimes they'd stand and punch one another, and other times they'd have their backs on the ground, rolling like a pack of pups. All the skill was in the hips. They trained for hour upon hour, in the heat of summer, until they were shimmering wet and sick. The men were a team. They'd never fight each other. They trained to fight other teams, conjured grudges against other men. When invited, they'd fight one on one, in 'the cage', which was not a cage but a fence-lined eight-sided octagon dropped in the middle of a casino, or a gym, or sometimes a strip club. They'd pound and writhe until a man gave up, a man passed out, or three five-minute rounds came to an end. It was legal, mostly.

Among the marvels of these men was how little they minded the presence of a writer in their midst. Most people change under observation, blink twice before answering, scan the treeline for words that won't offend. The fighters, in their insistent solidity, lacked the flickering feel of people looking to run. It came across as an open-eyed kindness, a heaviness of presence that made listening possible.

The first time I met them, Rob and Lonnie were days away from a fight in Des Moines. Rob was a pint-sized, red-haired former paralegal turned, when his lawyer lost his license, dump-truck driver.

'What does that entail?' I asked.

'You have a truck, you pick stuff up, you dump it,' he said. I wrote that down.

Lonnie was a thirty-something house painter whose extreme shyness others took for a terrifying masculine reticence. Cedar

Rapids feared him. We exchanged no words, ever.

The summer I met them they were training seven days a week, four hours a day. The idea was that your pre-fight training be more intense than the longest possible fight, which is to say five rounds and twenty-five minutes of pounding. I watched Rob thrust mounted men off his hips until he threw up, Lonnie whack a bag until he wept.

This was for the fight with the Tai Dam, a Southeast Asian tribe who'd traded Vietnam for the Midwest when the Americans shipped off. The problem with being resettled to the United States is that there are many of them, and one of them is Iowa. The Tai Dam endured in Des Moines, worked at Wells Fargo, raised sons who staged fights on the side. Rob was nursing a grudge against the whole tribe.

'They called me an Asian-stealer,' Rob said.

'They're Tai Dam. Your girlfriend is Japanese,' I said. 'It's different.'

'Doesn't matter,' he said.

'Maybe she's a Caucasian-stealer.'

'I am fighting,' Rob said, fist lifted all mock indignation, 'for interracial relationships!'

I loved these men, their embrace of pain, their sense of significance. They treated their bodies like some exotic animal they'd found fast asleep, beings they needed to wake to truly know.

The year before I became pregnant, my husband and I abandoned Iowa for Houston. He would study story-making in a fine arts program funded by oil magnates, and I would feed us while he finished. Houston felt like a vacation I'd taken by accident, perhaps a trip I'd won on talk radio. Real life was somewhere else, a place with fewer non-native palm trees and more friends.

I spent months job-searching, alone, hungry for human contact. I watched television on a stained couch in a one-room apartment, wishing I could drive to a coffee shop but unable to afford the coffee, anxious about the cost of gas. A wealthy neighborhood abutted ours, and when I could stand it no more I walked the streets. The houses were stucco with turrets. What does one do in a Houston turret? I imagined silk-clad women leaning languorously against curved walls, shooting pricey salves onto pursed lips. Thousands of feet beneath us, quivering droplets of oil encased in rock waited to be sucked to the surface by wells dipping and lifting like giant drinking birds. If the fighters were here, I thought, I'd feel the release, the slight shake of the earth as each drop wrests itself free. In their absence, I stared at the meticulously clipped hedges of people who provided legal counsel for the people who bought and sold what others forced from the ground.

I came to believe that my failure to be happy in this city was a failure of will, and tried to maintain an air of ironic distance. As defenses go, it wasn't much, or in any case, wasn't enough. When I finally scored a phone interview, a heavy-breathing CEO asked me about my childhood, my feelings. 'What do you most fear?' he asked. 'What breed of dog are you? Tell me about your childhood.' I feared inauthenticity, loved pointers, I said. He cut me off as I described my parents' gentle neglect. 'I'm looking for a *hunter*,' he said. 'You're not a hunter.' For some reason, I thanked him. He hung up before I could finish.

Pregnancy was a relief, a project. It involved other people. Once a week we gathered at Katherine's: me and my husband, other couples. A girl in yoga pants came always with a salad, munched as Katherine talked crowning, colostrum. There were the requisite lesbians. They took notes. I did not need notes, because I'd memorized the lines. If you didn't have the baby by week forty-two, the doctor would prescribe Pitocin. If you did have the baby by week forty-two, but took more than twenty-four hours to labor, the doctor would prescribe Pitocin. If you took Pitocin, the contractions would be super-sized, and you'd need the needle to the spine. If you accepted the needle, you'd be flat on your back, too numb to push, and they'd search out the scalpel so as to be home in time for *Law & Order: SVU*. Your baby would emerge drugged, overfull of fluid, deprived of healthy vulvar bacteria, denied his rightful microbiome.

It was 2014, and the biome was all the rage. We'd turned against overeager soaps, against bacteria-blasting translucent goo. Meta-studies suggested we'd do better to feed our children dirt, let them chew on shoe-bottoms lest their overscrubbed homes subject them to allergies, to asthma. Hospital interventions involved antibiotics. If you let them, they'd blast away the bacteria.

Katherine enveloped us in dolls, diapers, birth-journey DVDs. Watch the pregnant Mexican woman walk naked into the crisp river. She leans on her husband, a sensitive Japanese sculptor. Sun baked children play on the banks. Hear her moan, hear the children shriek, see her eyes roll back. A baby, born into warm Mexican microbes, protected, by its attractive and sensuous parents, against peanut allergies.

In the DVDs, women unleashed screams, caught babies in dirt huts, in baths, on suburban decks. ('Tell the neighbors first,' advised the deck people.) That you know something to be propaganda does not necessarily steel you against its narrative pull. I loved these videos, these women who swayed and stretched, who writhed desperately and rolled with opponents invisible. At the moment of delivery, a change of mood: a ferocious agony slakes to celebration. I cried every time.

We watched hospital births too, women in hospital-issued slippers still and supine, leashed to machines. Katherine's own first birth went like this. 'Your hips are small,' said the doctor, scheduled a C-section, numbed her up, sliced her open on a rolling bed. For 'small hips', she would risk blood clots, infection, a bladder accidentally snipped on the way in. The wound was such that she needed a wheelchair to get to her child, whom the hospital had placed in a translucent box. 'Explain this to me again,' she asked the doctor. 'Stop obsessing,' he snapped. Her next three were born in this living room, the siblings gathered round some spiritually significant quilt.

A spouse was a 'nest-builder'. Contractions came as 'tides', and after them, your vagina would be 'a sleeve'. Katherine was rational, skeptical, sarcastic and into metaphors. She had answers. I did not know how to change a diaper, dull my nausea or convince my nipple to withstand an infant's will to suck. I did not know how to labor. 'You're not supposed to know,' Katherine said. 'In the past, the tribe knew. Older women in the tribe would have taught you.'

That seemed right. I had been denied a tribe. I was a tribeless victim of modernity, marooned in Houston with my husband, alone in a world excessively obedient to standard medical practice.

'What tribe?' asked someone else's husband.

'The tribe that conveys culture from one generation to the next,' said Katherine.

'Yes but specifically, to what tribe are you referring?' He was Indian, accented, resistant to the rhetorical.

Katherine smiled. 'The one you don't have.'

The way you avoided Katherine's situation was this: you didn't let them make you docile. You didn't take off your cotton clothes, let them sheathe you in paper. They would try to stick a needle in your wrist and leave it hanging there, so that the IV the epidural required would be just a snap away. You would, submerged in a pain-induced mania, have to deny those who would pull you out.

I finally fell into a job as an underpaid fashion editor at a glossy Houston magazine, where I worried over blog posts with titles like 'Gingham Goes Glam' and 'Hair Chalk: What's the Deal?' I spent nights at runway shows held in car dealerships, wrote roundups in which fashion people were 'mixing and mingling', enjoying 'light bites'. I hired models and makeup artists, borrowed $7,000 scarves from gay shopkeepers. The magazine's editor asked that we book an eighteen-year-old fashion photographer Houston deemed a 'boy genius'. The boy dimmed the lights, draped the models in sequins, adorned them in broken mannequin parts. I could see that the plastic arms approximated a solemnity he thought befitting of his genius, made him feel connected to something. Oil quivered beneath our feet, and neither of us could feel it. He picked up a disembodied torso.

'No torso,' I said, 'stick to the limbs.'

He shook his head in disgust. 'I'm trying to *tell a story*,' he said.

When a fighter forces another man's arm into an unbearable twist, he calls it a 'submission', one man conceding to another. But in years of following fighters I have come to see submission as something that happens the moment they walk into the cage, trading the angsty disquiet of self-protection for the broadening promise of great pain. Let others worry about cavities and smile lines and slowly clogging capillaries. You can fight entropy, or swim in it.

That spring, after one dark evening of mixing and mingling, I surrounded myself with happy artifacts of my past life: a motley pile of journals, bookmarked with torn tickets to strip-club fights. I wrote about the Tai Dam, about Rob trotting into the octagon, about the night he had fallen almost immediately to a rain of punches, froze, choked, 'failed', in fighter terms, 'to defend'. The sound of his body hitting the mat was surprisingly slight. The fight lasted fifty-four seconds. Interracial couples would maybe need a new defender.

There were nine fights that night, and Lonnie's was the last. The referee waved and Lonnie, slim and sculpted, laid into his opponent, kicked him in the stomach, jabbed him in the jaw. Lonnie absorbed an achingly precise blow to his orbital bone, and slammed the man to the mat. Both men landed on the ground, sweat-soaked, kick-flailing until they found a way up.

They struggled to gain purchase, lying on top of each other. Once, on television, I saw a 200-pound tuna dragged aboard a small boat. Stunned, it was still for a moment, until it opened its mouth and revealed its razor teeth. A single slim muscle thrashed and whacked, slamming sailors, snapping them into the water. It's that fish I think of when I see two men on the ground, willing their bodies into a single sleek substance that will knock the other man flat.

By round five Lonnie was supine on the ground, the man sitting atop him. 'Hip out!' Rob screamed from outside the cage. 'Hip out!' The man punched Lonnie just below the right eye. He took blow after blow to the same soft square of skin between the lower lashes and the top of the cheekbone. It was tearing, rivering red into the corner of the eye. All Lonnie needed to do was tap the mat, offer the slightest flick of his wrist, to concede the fight and end the assault. 'Elbow him!' shouted Rob uselessly. He was just a foot away, but Lonnie had given himself over to a place words can't penetrate. Again and again during those years, I watched men swim through some portal violence opened for them. They came back ecstatic and whole.

The bell rang, the mood broke, and everyone cheered. Lonnie had lost. He stood up smiling, a racing stripe of blood across the top of his shaved head.

Afterward, the team gathered around Lonnie, now flat on his back on a stretcher waiting for the fight doctor to conduct his post-fight exam. A purple egg rose from his brow, the suggestion of a split bone under the surface. He smiled, and his gums shimmered pink and wet, except where they were red with blood. Together the tribe recounted the fight, shouting 'Warrior!' and 'Beast!', words of praise for the man who made them proud. They were giddy, and he was both with them and not, absorbing their admiration while riding his own high somewhere far off.

This baby would not have a leather-bound bouncer, a stroller with Wi-Fi, none of the luxuries I saw on wish lists made public by prosperous parents of the child's cohort. We were writers, and he would suffer for it. We lacked loving extended families, and he would suffer for that too. He'd have a mother with an unpublished manuscript on fighters, and a father in graduate school. I wanted him to have his rightful microbiome, which I imagined as a living second skin, a shield of spores to ward off future hurts. I wanted, desperately, to give that to him, to be brave enough to resist the saline lock, the numbing needle. I'd take the hit so he'd be a step ahead, submit myself to the pain and preserve what was his.

Afternoons at Katherine's lasted three hours. We seemed always to be talking around the point. The point was: How could I be more like Lonnie? 'Try some birth tea,' said the books. 'Go to yoga.' I went to yoga. 'Follow your blissipline,' the yogi said. 'Try a mantra. Say: "My body knows what to do. My body knows what to do."'

Pregnancy is a pack activity. All across the country, my friends were with child. Four of the five had midwives, doulas, books by Ina May. 'You will think you are going to die,' someone advised a friend of mine in search of a midwife. 'Find the person you want to see when you're going to die.' Katherine collected birth stories on her website, testimonials from mothers with whom she'd moaned. 'I was sure that my hips were being smashed in half. I screamed and screamed,' wrote one woman. 'Katherine looked me dead in the eyes and said, "*I know*."'

I wanted to argue with someone, so I called my mother, who thought drug refusal was madness. ('It will hurt,' she pointed out.) I leafed through the *Lancet* and lectured her about the 'cascade of interventions'. I used the term 'vacuum extractor'.

The hospital was a glass-and-steel building huddled with dozens of other such structures in a 'medical complex' the size of a city. The outdoor space between the buildings was hard dead emptiness, unused but for soft doctors spiriting between them. Inside, a series of elevators led to my own doctor, a young and plump Punjabi woman I liked, mostly because she reminded me of television's Mindy Lahiri. 'I think you should consider a *vaginal birth*,' she said at our first visit, as if this was an experimental treatment she'd read about somewhere.

Mindy loved the magazine for which I worked, and thought me an authority on glam gingham styles. She and I regarded each other with a kind of wary adversarial respect. I said I wouldn't be getting an epidural, and she nodded knowingly. Like hadn't she heard *that* before.

'I'd like to try a water birth.'

Her hospital promised 'jetted tubs', which was why I had chosen it.

'You can labor in the tub,' she said, meaning, not *deliver* in the tub, for legal reasons she claimed not to comprehend.

This was the moment when my unwritten birth plan sprung into being. It was: Resist getting out of the tub. What were they going to do? If they came at me, I would flail in a way that looked fetus-endangering. What did the lawyers have to say about assaulting a woman in labor? A lot, I imagined.

On the hospital tour, in a model birthing room, I learned that the saline lock, the plastic stick that stays poking out of your wrist, is compulsory. I did not want a sharp object piercing my wrist skin as I writhed, did not want to be one step closer to tapping out. It was, the tour guide said, 'hospital policy'. 'With whom can I discuss this?' I asked, emphasizing *whom* on the off chance that grammatical precision might denote authority and impel this tour guide to lead me to the breathing font of hospital dicta, an actual body with blood and gums and delicate ear bones that would twitch in tune to whatever I might say about the sanctity of the microbiome. I wanted her to take me to the source.

She shrugged, I smiled and as we walked away our heels clicked on the eleventh floor of a glass-and-steel box.

I was deep in a pre-bed downward dog when my water broke. It was late, and my husband was reading *The Sun Also Rises*. 'Read it aloud,' I said. This was the nest I needed. I breathed through Jake's manly longings, his absurd inarticulate angst. I thrilled at the first tightening, the womb gone hard, a slack bag turned firm. I liked ceding control to some process, as if lodged within a tracked car wash, sitting and waiting for the spray. My body knows what to do.

The pain nipped up my legs, my back, my hips. I would miss this particular pain for months afterward, long for its pert insistence to pull me from the drift. I had read that it was like a wave, but it was not like a wave. The takeover was not gradual. It was a dominating possession that came all at once and fell away as if I'd dreamed it.

Early morning in the hospital, I am many hours without sleep, leaning on walls, crying into Katherine's breast, shrieking on occasion. I am in a black cotton dress, having refused the paper one. I have been told to picture a flower opening and closing with each successive contraction. It is not like a flower. It is a single slim muscle, thrashing its way through my ribs. The fish careens from side to side as if carried by waves, whacks me onto my knees. It rests. In a moment, it will come back stronger.

I curl up on the bed. Prior to this I had always imagined extreme pain as pointed, the rip of skin above Rob's eye, the sharp crack of his nose bone. But the sensation of a blunt ballooning fury, of some rib-rending force awakening inside the cage of you? Also bad.

A young doctor, not Mindy, arrives. She is wearing the glasses of a girl who affects interest in anime. She does not care about the microbiome. She says it's time for a saline lock, 'just in case something happens down the line'. Her manner suggests that I would definitely want to go numb later, that she knows this, that this attempt to go without is a waste of her time. I beg to be left alone. I want to be able to move.

'It's hospital policy,' she says, her smile tight. 'In case we need it later.'

The fish wants to thrash my hips apart, split them like a wishbone. Its razor teeth seize on a back rib, the second one down.

'No,' I say.

'Did you discuss this with your doctor? Do you have permission for this?' she asks.

'Yes,' I lie.

She leaves for an hour, returns when I am leaning against Katherine, driving my head into her shoulder. She says that Dr Mindy denies my story. 'It's hospital policy,' she says. 'I'm ordering it.'

My husband and Katherine look at each other. The doctor stares at me in open challenge. From somewhere deep in my consciousness, a phrase rises up, words I maybe heard in a movie, words I maybe heard on *SVU*.

'I do not consent,' I say.

The phrase unlocks something. Her lips tighten; dark lines gather around her mouth. She sighs heavily, looks ostentatiously sad. Then she forces a smile. 'This is for your own safety,' she says, 'because we want the best for you.' Witnessing this are a passel of nurses, eyes on the ground.

'I do not consent.'

I do not consent. I do not consent. I do not consent. The doctor with the glasses has stopped smiling. She shakes her head, mutters something about talking to other doctors and leaves the room. It is 6 a.m.; I have missed a night of sleep. The fish feeds on my fatigue. It chaws at some organ, ripping meat from bone. It swims in a sloppy spiral, faster and faster, pummeling ribs as it circles. It rarely rests now. I think, maybe if I open my mouth wide enough, it will propel itself outward. My body knows what to do.

The pain is gathering. I am worried about time now, worried that they will blast the biome and slice me open if I don't hurry. Katherine has to leave to get her kids to school, but she thinks I am many hours from opening, and she will be right back. For a short period of lacerating torment, the fish rips down through my womb and swims back up to beat against my ribcage.

My husband is saying something, but I can't make out what it is. Instead, I hear the fish. He has the voice of a man. His gums are pink and wet, his razor teeth red with my blood. He smiles a far-off smile, a smile of deep and abiding calm. It's Lonnie's calm, some sacred high only known through agony. If you can dwell here long enough, I am sure, there is some knowledge to be had, some grotesque erasure of the self that makes knowing possible. Only then the bloody yank from pain to pleasure, that glorious tempo shift not known among the numb. I want to come back from knowing what it is that Lonnie knows, and I can almost see my way there, like a memory I'm muscling my way toward, while the fish clubs my tailbone.

I need an epidural.

I say to my husband: I need an epidural. Katherine is gone. There is panic in his face; does he listen to the me deranged by pain? I feel sorry for him. I think: Press forward. Convince him that you are fit for self-governance. Try to form normal-sounding words. Are you sure? Are you sure? I am sure. There is no skill in my hips.

The nurse comes back in. Are you sure? I am sure. She reaches inside. In the past ten minutes, the ones where I lost my nerve, the body has opened. You are so close, she says. Perhaps you can make it just a little longer? But something has snapped shut for me. Am I sure? I am sure.

The doctor with glasses comes back, nodding, smiling, a show of magnanimity as the world arranges itself in precisely the pattern she expected. She says the words 'saline lock'. She says the words 'hospital gown'. I stare at the bed as the nurse stabs my wrist. I twist sideways, and a bearded anesthesiologist, sounding bored, tells me to be still. I continue to scream. He rolls his eyes. He stabs the fish dead.

Relief is sudden and total. A sense of the sacred, of the elemental, is a fragile thing. It has already slipped out of the room.

My husband and I chat happily. Katherine arrives, and doesn't judge. My phone rings, and my husband answers it. 'I was supposed to interview that guy,' I say. 'Tell him I'm in labor.'

Numb from the waist down, flat on my back, I text emoji to my mother. I progress. When it's time, Dr Mindy arrives, chatting, smiling, with an entourage a dozen women deep. I ask my husband to turn up the music, and nurses sway their hips in time with the tune. The tribe makes itself. A single push, and the baby swims out, sleek and wet.

Back when I was deep in the writing, when a child would have been unthinkable, friends, fight fans, asked me about my book. The fighters never asked, except once, on a night when I was three vodkas in and holed up alone in a Vegas hotel. The text was from the team's leader, a fighter for whom the fight was an opportunity to philosophize.

'How do you see us?'

The query filled me with fear. I sat up in bed, stared at the phone, decided, because I was drunk, to tell the sober truth.

'I want,' I typed, 'what you have.'

In the fighters I witnessed a liberating annihilation I envied. At Katherine's, we watched women loose themselves from the ordinary world, rip through a wall impenetrable but for moments of extraordinary violence. 'Microbiome,' we said. 'Vacuum extractor,' we said, because we had no words for whatever lay beyond the lacerating spasms of agony to which we aspired. That you fear to name your need, that you ascribe your desire to maternal altruism rather than human curiosity, does not mean it is wrong to want what you want. I still think it noble, this experiential wanderlust, this drive to get to a place I in my weakness will never know.

I am saying that it was never about the baby. I am saying that it didn't have to be. ∎

Poem Conveyed

I can't say which ghost
not because I am being coy
and not because the ghost
is being coy. In the glut
of ghosts, it is hard to tell
who is speaking. I do recall
a conveyor (the ghosts
call conversations 'conveyors'
as that is how they travel)
when someone
told me I ought to read
Alexander Pope
because he was disabled.
And I thought: Oh no,
now Pope will warm my pillows
and pollute my dreams.
He does not speak, directly,
in the poems about it.
Pope, you could say,
conveys scoliosis
in heroic couplet,
sleight of hand, anything
to escape his body.
And now that he is body-less,
he speaks through us.
You could say. Although
I myself have not caught
a Pope. Not that I know of.

© SAM CALDWELL

THIS IS NEW

Marc Bojanowski

Shortly after I lost my job teaching, I began taking my daughter on walks through the rural cemetery near the housing tract where we lived. We'd walk at dusk to watch the crows arrive from all corners of our small city, thousands of them, all reptile black and shiny, all cronking and cawing, a regular murderers' row of motion and noise.

'They're settling in,' I'd tell my daughter, my breath showing white in the October cold. 'They're going nighty-night.'

She'd take her dimpled fist from her mouth and point her tiny finger up at the birds and say, 'Quo, Daddy. Quo.'

And in her toddler's voice I would momentarily forget that I'd lost my job and shamed myself and humiliated our family; I would forget that I'd become a stay-at-home dad and that my wife was supporting us financially; I would forget that what I had done to be fired isn't done and gone and won't be because it's alive and haunting and available on the Internet; and in that guttural 'Quo, Daddy. Quo', I would forget that none of this would have happened if I'd just taken a deep breath, suppressed my emotions and said to the young woman, 'Leave. Now.'

We walked each evening to watch the crows roost, but also so my wife could try to relax after a long day at work. We left her alone because it pained me to see her exhausted after sitting in front of a computer screen all day. Her clothes were rumpled, her hair was graying prematurely and her eyes harbored a weariness compounded by the pressures of having to be our sole source of income during the Great Recession.

I hated being responsible for her misery. I wasn't an alcoholic deadbeat loafer. I wasn't cheating on her. I wasn't wallowing in self-pity at having to take on the responsibilities of fatherhood in my late twenties, a time when most of my friends were still dating or were only recently engaged and still enjoying the benefits of double incomes and no kids during a severe economic downturn.

While my wife made enough to cover our mortgage, car payment, utilities and grocery bills, she did not make enough to cover those expenses *and* childcare, and the jobs that I might find, if I were lucky, in that economy, would not enable her to quit her job so that she could care for Cordelia while I worked. As a result, I became a stay-at-home dad.

The trouble started with the young woman during the second week of the fall semester. One day in class she brought out her cell phone after I had dimmed the classroom lights to show a documentary.

'Why don't you put that away,' I said, but not forcefully, not wanting to single her out as a young black woman in a class of Latino and white students.

'I've already seen this one before,' she said.

'Well, watch it again. It's important.'

'Not to me it isn't.'

'Your grade's not important?' I asked her.

'Don't put that on me. I'm here to learn.'

'Well, let's learn.'

'This isn't learning. This is you telling me what to think, not how to think better.'

I was stunned.

The classroom was dark except for the light of the television, but I could feel the students' eyes on me, and I hoped they couldn't see that I was blushing.

She wasn't some dumb kid mouthing off; she was bored. I was boring her. I wasn't reaching her mind.

A classroom is a curious place. Most of us have experience in them, but comparatively few of us have experience at the head of them. We're the ones who know it all and who are frequently wrong because we have so many opportunities to be. We know what's best for our students and each of us knows better than the other instructors what's best for everyone else. We are, often to a fault, well intentioned, and our petty squabbles and ancient animosities play out in hallways and copy rooms, in snarky email chains and blind carbon copies. We bad-mouth and backstab, and the students we grade, they know it.

I taught because there's nothing like that feeling when someone fully understands something complicated because of something you've articulated and demonstrated over time. That feeling is addictive. It is, in the old sense of the word, awesome.

When the economy collapsed and the houses around us emptied in foreclosure, the people who moved out left trash in the yards and sometimes they even left their cats. Along with a family of Chinese immigrants and a house shared by two Mexican families, we were the last ones on the street. It was us and the cats and their kittens. In two years, the only person to move into the subdivision was a twenty-one-year-old white kid with dreadlocks who bought a house at auction, paid with cash and immediately set up a marijuana grow operation in the garage.

Some nights, when our heads were still above water, my wife and I would put Delia down early and sit on the front porch and watch the cats pick through the trash while the crows came over the rooftops through the reds and golds of a smoggy sunset on their way toward the cemetery. The air smelled of woodsmoke and fabric softener. Rivets on jeans tinked, tumbling smooth along the inside of our laundry dryer drum. We'd sit and sip white wine and watch kittens roll over one another in the thick nap of unmowed lawns.

'It's so surreal,' we'd say to each other.

But it wasn't surreal at all. What it was was that we could afford the mystery then. We could afford the surreal nature of skinny toms fighting in pools of street-lamp light. We were the young couple with the baby. Young professionals starting a family and weathering the downturn. I was the proud father who taught composition at the local community college; my wife worked for an environmental restoration non-profit. We were both out to save the world. We were comfortable in our selves, in our marriage, in the scents and sounds and sense of the luxuries of our class.

The young woman was a nineteen-year-old foster child with severe dyslexia and cigarette scars along the undersides of her forearms. In her journal she described the scars 'like a row of tiny gray buttons'. She kept them hidden beneath the long sleeves of sweatshirts, the cuffs of which she kept gathered in the palms of her hands. She was a young black woman with an expensive cell phone her foster mother had bought for her. The mother wanted to shower the young woman with gifts because she was wealthy and kind-hearted and well intentioned. The young woman had nothing but loving things to write about her foster mother.

The night before the incident I had slept poorly because Cordelia was up with a fever and my wife and I had been arguing about a refi I wanted but she didn't. Then, that morning, I drank too much coffee on an empty stomach and I was irritable and unwell. Finally, when the young woman refused to put away her phone after I asked her to and when she began navigating the backside of the phone with her thumb and lifting it like she was going to record my response I stepped forward and slapped the phone from her hand. I stepped forward and only when I felt my hand smack her hand and heard the phone clatter did I realize what I had done. I felt it all the way up my arm, cold and liquid and metallic, up to where it nestled in my shoulder and ached warmly. And, in that instant, I knew my career as a teacher was over.

I dreamed last night that a meteor passed dangerously close to Earth. Caught in our gravitational pull, it made a complete loop around our small planet before slinging itself back out into space. Like a giant magnet held up to a hard drive, it erased entire servers, databases. We lost photos and bank accounts and emails. Televisions flickered and calls got dropped. The entire electronic storehouse was gone, and I was free.

'Nice description,' I used to write in pencil in the margins of my students' essays, 'but avoid abrupt shifts in tense.'

After I slapped the young woman's hand, my ears were ringing and the students were on the verge of riot. The young woman was on her feet, held back by two young men. She was shoving her hand out at me and spitting her words she was so angry. The spittle landed on my cheek. That night, I couldn't bring myself to look in the mirror when I washed it away.

Three days later, my wife and I went to the local superstore to buy Cordelia a box of diapers and a sippy cup. On our way out, we stopped for coffee at the franchise situated near the sliding-glass entrance and exit to the superstore, and we took a table near one of the beige fob detectors where we sat breathing that bitter mixture of parking-lot air and roasted coffee and off-gassing plastic.

I looked at my wife, sitting across the small table from me. Her eyes were red from lack of sleep and her cheeks splotchy; I hadn't brushed my teeth in days and my mouth tasted of iron and rot.

'We're going to make it,' she said. 'We'll be fine.'

'I'm sorry,' I said to her.

She took my hand, resting on the table, squeezed it and said, 'I know.'

And that was when I heard my voice for the first time. It was my voice but not my voice, not anymore. Delia was in my lap, reaching for my cup of coffee, just out of reach, and the entire world existed for me in the flecks of gold in her tiny green eyes. When I heard my voice I was looking down into her eyes and then up at my wife, who was watching two young women several tables over. The young women were hunched over a phone, and something about their postures – I can't describe it; the cant of their necks, perhaps, something – indicated that I was somehow involved in what they were watching.

'How many times do I have to tell you to put that thing away?' I heard my voice emanate from the phone. 'You're distracting me from doing my job.'

'Don't come any closer.'

'Then put it away.'

'I'm hella gonna record this.'

'Put. It. Away.'

'Don't tell me what to do, white boy.'

And then the sharp sound of the slap, followed immediately by the hand-to-mouth *whoa* of the students in unison; a dense, singular sound that wakes me roaring some nights from sleep.

That spring, Cordelia and I stood beside an apple tree in bloom while watching a crow pick walnut meat from a halved hull it had dropped to the center of the street from up on a black, sagging power line.

This is what we did mornings after chores of laundry and cleaning and baths. I packed a diaper bag with food and water, a bottle of breast milk tucked in a beer coozie and a sippy cup with watered-down apple juice. White petals clung to the stroller's black wheels, to concrete gutters dappled with oil spots.

We were watching the crow pick with its dull beak at the walnut when I noticed from behind thick curtains of a downstairs window a small, old woman with a wrinkled, round face. She was peering at me around the edge of the curtain, her tiny finger hooking a curtain fold, which she released as soon as I noticed her.

I sensed what she was thinking before the front door opened and she waddled down the walk to speak it. It was on my mind most days anyway.

'What're you doing here?' she asked me.

'We're watching the crow.'

'Where's the girl's mother?'

'She's at work.'

'Why aren't you at work?'

'I lost my job.'

'So get a new one.'

'It's not that easy these days.'

'Sure it is. You just do it.'

'Quo, Daddy. Quo.'

The woman's eyes narrowed. 'There's boys dying in Iraq,' she said.

'I know.'

'And what're you doing?' She raised her bony hand, the back of it a network of raised veins and liver spots, pointed it at me, and said, 'Pushing a stroller.'

'Quo, Daddy. Quo.'

'I'm a teacher,' I responded.

'Oh,' the woman grinned, 'that explains it.'

That night, I walked two miles to a bar and got drunk by myself. When I told the bartender what I did for a living, he told me a joke: 'Daddy Bear's at home slaving over the stove when Momma Bear comes home from work and Baby Bear comes home from school. They all sit at the table, and Momma Bear says, "This porridge is too hot." And Baby Bear says, "This porridge is too cold." And Daddy Bear undoes his apron, and says, "Shut the fuck up, both of you, and eat."'

Understandably, my union abandoned me completely. Long criticized for protecting negligent and ineffective faculty, this was an opportunity to take a stand publicly, to demonstrate those things that they did not tolerate. The story and video had gone viral. The aggregates posted links. A white male teacher had struck a female student of color. Firing me was, in the words of the union president, 'a no-brainer'.

One Saturday night a week or so after the incident, I slunk into the English Department to collect my things and to return the key to my office. In my mailbox there was a slip of college-ruled binder paper, neatly folded and addressed to me. It was, I knew immediately by the handwriting, the work of a young woman who had been a student of mine in a developmental class several semesters prior. She would frequently write poetry on the backs of her assignments. Sometimes the poems were in Spanish, and at home at night my wife and I would use our high-school Spanish and an online dictionary to translate them.

'Beautiful,' I would write beside the poems, 'but let's focus on your fragments.'

Occasionally, this young woman would come by my office to ask me to look over her essays, but more I think to show off how much she'd improved than to ask for my help. On the backs of her assignments, I noticed, she still wrote poetry.

I unfolded the slip of paper and there, at the center of the page, were three short lines, evenly spaced and without punctuation.

> ripples regard less
> farther from their source
> they smooth

No caps. Not one period or comma. Still, pure meaning, sentenced to the page.

That summer, a stray tomcat bit the hand of the young man running the marijuana grow down the street. He'd been feeding the cat nightly and, when he reached down to pet it, it bit into his hand and stayed clamped there as he attempted to shake it loose.

The young man's hand swelled to twice its normal size and the next morning, when he went to the emergency room, they stuck a needle down through the swelling, directly to the bones in his hand. Eight times they did this as a precaution against rabies. Eight times in each tooth mark.

'Hurt like fuck,' he told me, smoking a joint. 'You want?' he offered, holding his breath.

'Why not?' I said. 'It's not like I got work tomorrow.'

Later, when I told my wife what had happened to him, she shook her head and her eyes began to water. I wrapped my arms around her shoulders and pulled her to my chest.

'We don't have to live here anymore,' I said bravely.

She pushed back from me. Back, but not away.

'Where will we go?' she asked, her eyes prying at the space beyond mine.

'We can live anywhere you want.'

She shook her head ever so slightly, her eyes smiling now, but smiling at me with pity because I had yet to understand what she'd known since the beginning.

'This is never going to go away,' she said. 'You know that, right? We'll have to explain this to Delia someday.'

'It'll be long gone by then, babe.'

She looked me directly in the eyes, shifting her gaze from one eye to the other and back again, the faintest trace of her smile gone.

'People think you're a racist,' she said.

'But I'm not. You know that.'

'It doesn't matter what I think.'

'Honey, I'm sorry, but you're wrong about this.'

'No,' she said. 'I'm not. You think it's like it is with books in a library, but this is different. This is new.'

'You're tired, sweetheart,' I told her, and her eyes hardened.

'Yes,' she said. 'I am tired. I'm tired, and I'm right.'

In the end, we moved. We sold our home at a loss and we left.

I teach online now. I contacted a for-profit college out here and they allow me to use my initials and my wife's maiden name. I don't see my students and they don't see me. Our only contact is through carefully chosen words. It's not the same as being at the head of a classroom, but it's the work I believe I am meant to do.

And, it leaves time for me to walk with Cordelia. She has a tricycle now, and her little tongue can shape the 'r' in crow. We watch other birds, but the crows are her favorite. Mine too. At dusk, when the rooflines and power poles around us are slipping into silhouette, the birds hop into the shadows welling around the trunks of the trees where they roost, and it's as if they disappear there. It's almost as if they've been deleted. ∎

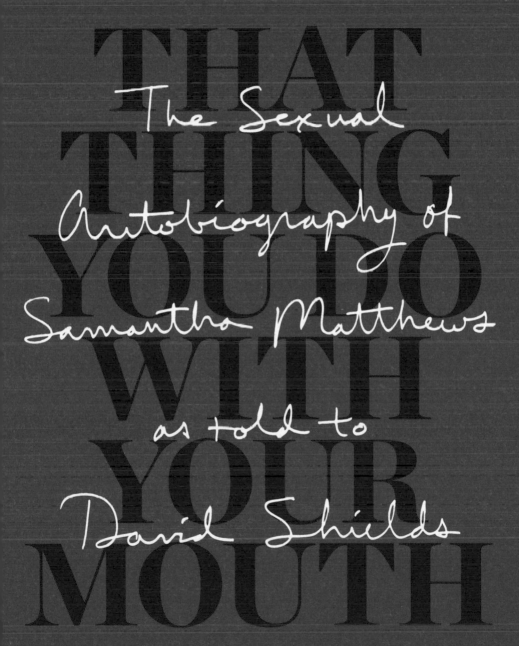

AN AGGRESSIVE INTERVENTION AGAINST
THE STANDARD TRAUMA-RECOVERY NARRATIVE

THAT
THING
YOU DO
WITH
YOUR
MOUTH

The Sexual Autobiography of Samantha Matthews as told to David Shields

AVAILABLE NOW FROM McSWEENEY'S

WILL THEY SING LIKE RAINDROPS OR LEAVE ME THIRSTY

Max Pinckers

Introduction by Sonia Faleiro

In India the pursuit of romantic love can be a dangerous thing. Contemporary lore is crammed with the bodies of men and women who refused to be fitted into socially expedient 'arranged' marriages. Young women have been doused in petrol and set alight. Young men, bones broken, have been thrown into suitcases. Reporting from the northern state of Uttar Pradesh recently, I interviewed a fifteen-year-old sitting patiently on her haunches as a relative rubbed a home-made whitening paste on her skin to prepare her for her wedding. She was three years below the legal age for marriage, but she was to be married the following day. Her parents said it was safest. Lustful men might kidnap her, they whispered. Or, she might fall in love.

I didn't meet a single person who had a 'love marriage' on my last trip to India, and whenever I have in the past, the fact is shared like a secret. It is loaded with melancholy, or fear, or defiance that begs to be unpacked. On an island in the Sundarbans archipelago, I once spent hours interviewing a vivacious schoolteacher named Toma Das. The only time a cloud fell over her face was when she spoke of her parents' attitude towards her husband, a factory worker. They disrespected him, she said. They implied she chose poorly because she chose for herself.

Still, the experience of falling in love is an anxiously desired state. Bollywood encourages this impulse. Before love, say our films, there is nothing, and to fall in love is to be born.

Max Pinckers deftly traps couples inside these two expressions of love: arranged love and film love. His brooding photographs show the hopelessness of some of these relationships, although they also display the rewards – expensive clothes, glinting jewellery, a white horse – because the ultimate reward of love for some isn't reciprocity but a wedding, and the security it represents.

In Pinckers's images the wedding clothes look stifling, as they often are in real life, and he has done well to pick up on this and to highlight the burden they may come to embody, with staging that resembles old-time Bollywood stills. Where some might see glamour in the artifice he has created, others will observe, perhaps from experience, drama and deceit.

The sense of suffocation goes beyond weddings, permeating the experience of Indians trying to express themselves romantically in a society where sexuality is feared. Love is little spoken of, and public expressions of love are taboo, so the idea of romantic love for young people is a constructed one. How one expresses love is not organic; rather, it is picked up in bits here and there – from films mostly, but also books, social media and porn – and pieced together to create a functional thing.

Since behaviour is also circumscribed by the smallness of shared living spaces, this piecing together, ironically, often takes place in public, and so Pinckers's lens transports us to an isolated seafront and what appear to be abandoned mills, capturing secretive smiles and dreamy glances. He enters claustrophobic living spaces as well, to show how a relationship between two typically ends up accommodating the needs of as many as a dozen – fathers, mothers, sisters, brothers. In one set of four images, a couple whispers intimacies on a narrow bed set against a paper-thin wall behind which people bustle about their day.

The hushed confidence, rather than laughter, or even an embrace, is a particular giveaway of a romantic relationship in India. The love here is furtive, quick and tense, and because of this it may appear comical to the outside gaze. But this is no comedy: the concealment of sexual love is a necessary skill, and it transcends class. To hide one's love – from embarrassment or from punishment – is a matter of survival for some. Love can be a chokehold, acknowledge a few of Pinckers's images – flames climb up a gauzy wedding dress in an allusion to dowry deaths; a noose fashioned out of a salwar kameez dupatta drops down from a ceiling fan. A newly-wed couple is shown with their faces rubbed out. But then the tightly entwined hands of another couple, clothes splashed with water, appear as though to say, No! Films are right. Love is a breathless, happy game.

As a reporter I'm naturally drawn to true stories, and in India love makes the news every day. It isn't spoken of as love, though; it is camouflaged in euphemisms. In April, as I sat at a restaurant in a small town in northern India leafing through a newspaper, I read about a young couple who ran off to marry, only to be caught by the police. The woman, eighteen, was engaged to another man – theirs was an arranged marriage – and days after she was made to return home she could have been the woman in Pinckers's photograph, dressed up in her finery amid a crowd of wedding guests. Her boyfriend was so desperate to break up the wedding that he wriggled into a skirt, stuck on a wig, slipped on some bangles and gatecrashed the wedding. The 'body language of the youth' gave away that he wasn't a woman, reported the *Times of India*, which went on to say that the young man was quickly arrested and jailed. The newspaper led their front-page story with the headline BOY DRESSES UP AS WOMAN, but of course the real story was that two people in love were torn apart by tradition.

Pinckers shares this fascination for true stories, and the photographs he has plucked out of newspapers and the Internet illuminate most clearly how hard it can be to be young and full of wanting in modern India. A set of screen grabs reveals comments posted by a young woman on behalf of her friend on the website of the Love Commandos, an organisation that claims to assist lovers under threat from family and social leaders. The woman's tone dials up from urgent to frantic: 'Its all bull shit!' [*sic*] she writes, in what appears to be her last email to the Commandos. 'She kept asking for help . . . But no one helped her. At last she finally killed herself today.' The woman's words collapse into an exhausted prayer. 'May her soul rest in peace.' ∎

bout my wish they stoped even talk me n its been 2 monts from den they didnt talk 2 me but earlier dis they usd to talk wid me daily. they are old enough n worked hard for us n our good life i dnt want to leave dem as well dnt want to ignore dem for my love. but they are not ready to talk bout dis matter. we can make anyone understand when the discusion happen on dat matter but how i make dem understand ifthey are not ready to talk about it. her mummy n elder brother are agree n her faher will never agree. n if we do court or love marriage he will definetli haress us by police n all means. in case if i will b jailed den idnt want my parents to be draged or being punished for my mistakes. plz help us for a safe n trouble free marriage............??????????
Thanking You
Akhilesh Yadav
#########

SAUMYA
June 16th, 2012   1:41 pm

I know that I am writing from the same account as my friend did. But we are different people. She called your helpline number and she was asked to send her address at your email. But aftr tat nothing happened. NO action. she didn't tell you to make her marry, she wanted your help just to take admission in that college where they would be together. She wanted you to rescue her from her suffocation that her parents have given her. But what did u guys do?..
She ate ********* and stuffs nd finally landed up in hospital with critical case. Please help her even now. I beg you.

SAUMYA
June 15th, 2012   4:02 pm

Its all bull shit!..If this site was actually capable to help love couples,then my friend wouldn't have died yesterday. She kept asking for help.You all can see her comments, her name is AAYUSHI ANAND. But no one helped her. At last she finally killed herself today. She died last night at 10:30 PM. May her soul rest in peace.
But as far as you all are considered, God will punish you for this crime. If you can't help others don't put up fake things and promises.

LoveCommandos.org
June 15th, 2012   9:47 pm

Dear Aayushi alias Saumya
You are posting your messages using different names. We understand that you may be stressed. You can call our Helpline number which is prominently displayed on our website.
Last night (14-Jun-2012), you posted messages at 11:10 PM and then at 11:21 PM and now you are posting using a different name.
You have posted these messages:
13-Feb-2011: http://lovecommandos.org/comment-page-1/#comment-33
11-Jun-2012: http://lovecommandos.org/comment-page-9/#comment-613
13-Jun-2012: http://lovecommandos.org/comment-page-9/#comment-625
14-Jun-2012: http://lovecommandos.org/comment-page-9/#comment-635
14-Jun-2012: http://lovecommandos.org/comment-page-9/#comment-637
14-Jun-2012: http://lovecommandos.org/comment-page-9/#comment-646
Please call our Helpline Number: 09313784375
We provide assistance in protecting couples, helping them fight harassment and giving them shelter so they can marry freely.
- Love Commandos -

---

atj
June 15th, 2012   10:07 pm

Sir/Madam
I am a keralite christian guy, aged 24. Parents settled in Mumbai. The girl I love is a keralite Hindu girl, aged 24. Even she and her parents are settled in Mumbai. I am done with my engineering from Mumbai and completed Masters from United States, looking for a job which I will be getting for sure in a month. She is currently doing her MBA from India and even she is an engineer already. By giving these details I just want to make u all sure that we both are educated with respective post graduations as well. So

95841-1

Original
on
econdary
08, Roll
by CBSE,
n actually
.No. B-101,
anda
or-56,
0040195860-1

, 39 Bunglow
Nagar, Delhi-
st 200 original
share
earing
umber 74802,
numbers
236915; certificate
401, distinctive
4176516-24176615.
ontact 9810159736.
0040195781-1

n Gupta S/o Bal
upta have lost my
llotment cum
n Letter of G-62,
clave, Pitampura,
contact at above
040195766-1

ny original
an Higher
n year 1977
ass out from
s been actually
itly A-97,
own-I,
9810894741.
0040195914-10

iginal Certificate
Roll No 8843088
2 Finder please
Manish S/o Tuk
r Resident Flat 1,
re Station C.P.
elhi 0040195848-1

otified for the
rmation that my Original
tificate of Main Secondary
hool Examination Year
01, Class-X, Roll No. 6146649
assed out from CBSE has
been actually lost. Finder
Contact: Tanuja Rohera,
11/58-A, Tilak Nagar, New
Delhi-110018. 0040195875-1

me
-3
o
tam

004-2
as
n
name
5825-1
akur
Colony,
ve
Bittoo
95760-2
ayan
ampus,
16,
e to
all
95727-1
ranjan
a,
ged
06004 1
c-10,
anged
bhijeet

LOST

I, Paramjeet Singh Address 6073/ 14-15, Bari Market, Sadar bazar, Delhi-110006, Lost My Registration No.07490363322 name of M/S Zipper Point. Finder May Contact at Above Address.

PUBLIC NOTICE

WE JINDAL ITF ,THE OWNERS OF THE BARGE MV PRADYUN HAVE LOST ITS ORIGNAL CERTIFICATE OF REGISTRATION HAVING OFFICIAL NO PNJ-615 IF SOMEBODY FINDS IT PLEASE RETURN TO JINDAL ITF LTD

Jindal ITF center, 28 Shivaji Marg New delhi-110015,India 91-1145021983-984

LOST AND FOUND

The Company- M/S. Vital Toolings Pvt. Ltd., having registered office in Delhi,has lost its Original Sale Deed of farm No. CR-18 in scheme known as Aravali Retreat, situated in and around village Raisina Tehsil Sohna Distt. G...

name to Prahalad Sharma.

PUBLIC NOTICE

This is to be informed to public at large on behalf of my clients Sh. Ravi Batra S/o Late Sh. Jai Dev Batra & Smt. Anita Batra W/o Sh. Ravi Batra R/o House no.-2175, Sector-12, Sonepat, Haryana, has disowned their son Sh. Tarun Batra & his wife Smt. Jyoti Batra and also debarred them from their movable and immovable properties. Hereinafter, my clients shall not be responsible for any act of their son and his wife in any manner. And, if any person deals with them then they shall themselves be sole responsible for that.

PARVEEN TYAGI (Advocate)
Ch. No. 309, W.Wing, Tis Hazari Courts, Delhi

PUBLIC NOTICE

Be it known to all that Property No. QD-59, Vishakha Enclave, Pitampura, Delhi-110034 belongs to my client Master Ishaan Sharda acting through and by the hand of his mother and natural guardian, by virtue of the Registered Will dated 18.07.2005 executed by his grand father Late S. C. Sharda, Advocate and is the subject matter of pending litigation titled "Master Ishan Sharda Vs. Sanjeev Sharda and others pending in the Court of Ms. Sukhvinder Kaur, Learned Addl. District Judge, Rohini District Courts, Delhi while defendants therein had conspired together and had illegally and clandestinely been attempting to deprive my client of the possession thereof or otherwise create third party charge over it. Any person or party dealing with them or taking any action relating to the said property or part thereof shall be doing so entirely at its own peril risk and responsibility without involving my client's right title and interest therein.

VIJAY KUMAR GOYAL (Advocate)
Ch. No. 230, W.Wing, Tis Hazari Courts, Delhi

PUBLIC NOTICE

Know all men by these presents that my client Smt. Omwati W/o Late Sh. Uttam Singh R/o N-151, Vishnu Garden, New Delhi-110018 do hereby disown and debar her daughter Preeti from her all movable and immovable properties with immediate effect because she married at her own, without permission of my client and her family. Presently she is residing separately. My client and her family also break all relations with her.

Anybody dealing with her or having any connection with her shall be doing so at at his / her / their own risk, cost and responsibility whatsoever. My client and her family will not be held responsible for any act, deed and things done by her.

Sd/-DAYA NAND, ADVOCATE,
RZH-694, Gali No.15, Raj Nagar-II, Palam Colony,New Delhi-110077

PUBLIC NOTICE

I Rachna Kwatra wife of Sh. Sanjay Kwatra R/o A-4, F.F. Sai Co-Operative G.H.S. Ltd. Sector-13, Rohini, Delhi do hereby solemnly affirm that I am married to Sh. Sanjay Kwatra, however I do not have any good relations with him now, I am owner of immovable properties i.e. A-4, F.F. Sai Co-Operative G.H.S. Ltd., Sec13, Rohini, Delhi. & one Plot No-520, Pkt-B-3, Sector-29, Rohini, Delhi and any other immovable and movable property like Jewellary and Cash lying in the bank. I and my parents are having no relations regarding any of the transaction of above said Sanjay with any person General Public at large qua my properties and in case any body deal with him, he himself will be responsible for the act and conduct of said Sanjay Kwatra son of Late Sh. Mela Ram Kwatra.

Umesh Kapoor (Advocate)
Chamber No 118, Distt. Courts, Karnal

"IMPORTANT

Whilst care is taken prior to acceptance of advertising copy, it is not possible to verify its contents. The Indian Express Limited ...

Actio
at th

EXP
NE

A
nals o
Singh
with c
pool n
In
day a
class a
India
whelm
side.
endar
with
sprink
Air In
ball w
3-1 w
tourn
Th
dent
Vikra
field v
in mid
sure o
little f
turn t
out a
crisp p
rest of
Halap
scorin
field g
getic,
throu
tral c
defen
playin
flicks
rushin
Th
forwa
while,
mover
to get
tions,
front
from
that D

C

FOR
Rafat
straig
ing 2-
ters N
C
onshi
to out
Snook
H
with c
of the

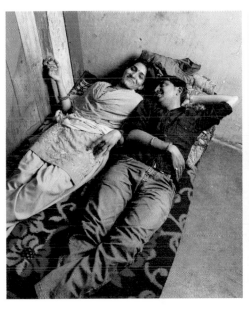
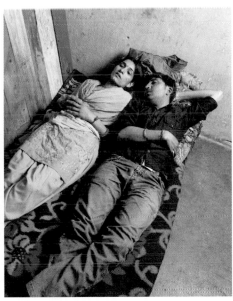

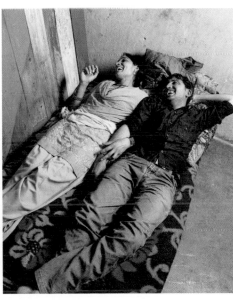

MP doc invents 'suicide-proof' ceiling fan

Manjari Mishra | TNN

Jabalpur: When German engineer Philip H Diehl invented the ceiling fan in 1892, he would have hardly imagined that his invention could end up being used as a tool to commit suicide. But there could soon be a remedy.

R S Sharma, a cardiology professor at the government medical college, Jabalpur, has invented a suicide-proof ceiling fan, which gets pulled down under additional weight leading to a soft landing of the person without stretching his neck or straining the noose. Sharma has applied for a patent and hopes it will be used in all homes and hostels. **P 12**

ADVT

HE IS A GREAT GUY – WISH TO MARRY HIM?

Tanya is my motorbike, and she's a beauty. I have always been a speed maniac !

Hi, my name is Din (Actually it was Dinshah. Yes, I'm a Parsi, but after I went to Canada and the U.S.A. I found that they could not pronounce our Indian names and eventually I cut my name short to Din and Oh Boy!

Did my poor Dad ever go through the roof, screaming and ranting that now I sounded like the neighborhood plumber!) I was married for many years until my wife was killed in a car accident about three years ago. Never having been the bachelor type, and with so much to offer to the right girl, I desperately want to find myself a wife.

When Dinshah runs I never watch him as I know he will win...

Before you waste your time reading through this entire advertisement, let me tell you the type of girl I want. Quite obviously you must speak English and have done your basic schooling. I don't care how much money you have or don't have. You should have a sense of adventure and the desire to live an exciting life. Be no older than 40 and slim. And please don't be a vegetarian. If you are divorced it doesn't matter, but definitely no children. I am much older than 40, but am very young at heart, very young physically, and very active, and any girl older than 40 would have a tough time keeping up with my active lifestyle.

I don't care how much money you have or don't have. You should have a sense of adventure and the desire to live an exciting life

Now let me tell you a bit about myself. I am from Mumbai and from my childhood days I was always very athletic. The year I left India I became the fastest 110-meter hurdler in the country! I ran for India against Russia in Uzbekistan in the trials for the Olympic Games. Throughout my school, college and University days I was an unbeaten Gymnastics champion. I often ran in front of ten thousand people screaming for me, but the head of the event would always say, "When Dinshah runs I never watch him as I know he will win. I WATCH HIS MOTHER!" My mother was my champion. She would jump up and yell and scream and wave her arms, and people sitting near her would grab her around her waist in case she fell over on the row in front! God bless her sweet soul, she was always my partner in crime!

FLYING

I first moved from India to Canada, and here I made a childhood dream come true. I learnt how to fly. At that time I was just a raw lad with three dollars in one hand and a suitcase in the other, but halfway through my training I made myself a very lofty promise that one day, some day, I would fly my own plane across the Atlantic Ocean to Europe and back. Yes, I've always had BIG dreams, but then I always work hard to make my dreams come true. Time passed, and in the years that followed I left Canada (too cold for me) and moved to Los Angeles. Met my wife and got married and started my own business. The business flourished and we did very well, and for fifteen years I kept that dream alive, never for a moment giving up on it. Finally, we sold my trusty single-engine plane and I bought a twin-engine plane (two engines), and in August of that year, with about thirty friends at our hangar, we flew off on what turned out to be the most beautiful adventure of my life!

We stopped in Greenland, Reykjavik, Iceland; Stavanger, Norway, then three more cities in Norway; Stockholm, Sweden; Copenhagen, Denmark; Amsterdam, Holland; Paris, France; London, England; then back to Reykjavic, Greenland and home. We took five weeks in all, met the most wonderful people, and the memories of that trip are still so real I can feel them even today.

There are lots of stories I have to tell you about this trip, and I'll do this one day when we are sitting quietly over a cup of coffee, or curled up side-by-side in a cozy bed. But for anyone out there who thinks it is easy to fly your own plane across the Atlantic, let me tell you it isn't! It is over 2,000 kms over the most dangerous ocean in the world. The U.S. Federal Government lists your chances of survival if you ditch into the ocean as two minutes! This is the main reason why one flies a twin- engine plane. The morning we left Reykjavik it was a grey and wet sky, and I had a huge knot in my stomach as I pushed the throttles forward for takeoff. Within minutes we entered clouds and flew blind for 90% of the flight. After about six hours my wife was dozing away and I was doing some calculations, thinking that we should be coming up on the coast of Europe very soon. Then, like pure magic, the clouds simply disappeared, we emerged into bright blue skies, and there in front of us was the green coast of Norway! We both screamed out loud and I had tears rolling down my face! After fifteen long years I'd made my dream come true! If this doesn't give you goose bumps you better go see a doctor!

TODAY'S PLANE

The plane I flew across the Atlantic was a Cessna 310 (I know, this means nothing to you). It is a sweet, simple plane, she flew that trip like a champion and I kept her for 17 years. By the year 2004, I was a much richer man than I was when we did our trip, and I finally decided to buy the type of plane that

only dreams are made of. The plane pictured here is my current plane, and if you don't think she is beautiful then once again you better go see a doctor! She is twin-engined, six seater, turbo-charged, and what makes her so unusual is that she is pressurised, which means I can fly as high as 25,000 feet without oxygen, just like an airliner. Let your imagination run wild for a moment, think of how much of the world is waiting for you and me with a plane like this. The whole of the U.S.A., Canada, the Caribbean, Mexico, South America and yes, even another transatlantic trip to Europe! **Come on, drop your inhibitions and come home with me, you'll never regret it.**

The plane pictured here is my current plane, and if you don't think she is beautiful then once again you better go see a doctor

MY HOBBY

By now you're probably thinking, "If I marry this crazy fellow, life certainly won't be dull! But what does he do when we're not checking out the countryside on his motorbike, or flying in the plane on a three-week vacation to Alaska"! Well, ever since I was a little kid my hobby was always AEROMODELLING, and as I grew so did the hobby as you can see from the picture of one of my planes. Unlike everyone else I know in this hobby who buys their planes from the store, I of course, have to be different! I design my own planes and then build them myself. This one has a 9-foot wingspan, and weighs 45 kilos.

They are powered by powerful gas engines and controlled by very sophisticated radio control units. They fly at an average of 130 kph, and my biggest and latest model is 10 feet in wingspan and weighs over 68 kilos. I give you these dimensions so you can realize that these are no toys. My wife used to love spending time side by side with me in my workshop as I built my models, and would often come up with an idea better than mine! If I can't get you interested enough to do the same thing then we're going to have a problem.

TANYA

Tanya is my motorbike, and she's a beauty. I have loved motorbikes ever since I was little. It took me two years of crying and begging and screaming and pleading to get my poor parents to buy me one. Now here I have to make a confession to you. I have always been a speed maniac ! I absolutely hate riding on the freeways in America because of their strict speed limits. What I love is riding in Mexico. Sure, they too have speed limits but they have so few cops that I can speed to my heart's content, and I usually cruise at between 160 – 200 kmph! And I have never got a speeding ticket yet. Almost all the cities in Mexico are beautiful, and though I've travelled much of the world I think some of the finest temples, churches and monuments are in Mexico. Over the past ten years I've done three big trips all alone, and been to every single major city in Mexico, including Guatemala and Belize. I'll make you one promise right now. I would never expect you to sit with me at these ridiculous speeds. Riding on the bike is beautiful, and I will only go as fast as you are comfortable. I've done over 80,000 kms of high-speed riding and now would much prefer to settle done with my wife behind me. I promise you you'll love it. Tanya is a beauty.

MY HOUSE - MY PALACE

As I mentioned earlier my business in Los Angeles did extremely well, and after only 11 years I had made enough money to retire rich for the rest of my life!! So that's exactly what I did, and overnight I sold my lovely house (at a huge profit), and sold the business (at another huge profit). One day as my wife and I were waiting for the sales to go through, I told my wife, "The next house we live in I want to build myself without any help whatsoever!" I told you, all my dreams are really BIG! She turned to me and said, "Don't be stupid, you can't build a house by yourself". With all the strict rules and regulations and restraints about building in the U.S.A., and with life being much simpler in Mexico, we bought a beautiful two-acre piece of land just outside HERMOSILLO, in MEXICO. Oh boy, I can just hear all of you saying, "OH, HE LIVES IN MEXICO !" With all the bad publicity Mexico is receiving in the press these days, I don't blame you for shaking your heads and saying, "No way Jose." But before you rush to any negative judgment, if things were really that bad do you think I would be living such a lovely life in Mexico ??

As you can see from the photo the house is stupendous. I designed it, I drew the blue-prints, and I took 5 years building every single aspect of it. While I was building, the local newspaper did a full-size spread on the front page. After the house was complete it has become a sort of landmark in the city, and the local TV channel did a one-hour program on the house and called it one of the most beautiful houses in Hermosillo. A few months ago the Mayor of Hermosillo had dinner at the house, and a couple of months before my wife died the American Consulate and his very pregnant wife came over and spent three hours with us. By the way Hermosillo is only 45 minutes south of the U.S. border in my plane.

YOU CAN'T GO WRONG!

Think of the fabulous life I'm offering you living abroad; having a plane and all the freedom that goes with it; living in a beautiful palace of a house; two fabulous cars, one of which will be yours; never having to worry about money; and a loving husband to whom you will always be his precious little princess! I absolutely swear to you I would never be unfaithful, and I could never ever be rough with you. My principal job will always be to make sure you are the happiest girl in the world. Compare this with your current life and what you can look forward to if you do nothing. **I'll tell you something from experience nothing comes to you in life if you just sit and wait for it to happen. You have to take that step forward, you have to sometimes take a chance, and you have to grab the opportunity when it stares you in the face!** I'm not so brazen to think that I am the only one here doing you the favor, you will be doing me a huge favor too, for everything I have means nothing to me if I don't have you to share it with.

I am staying at a prominent hotel at Churchgate, and friendly interviews will be conducted at THE REGUS CENTER, right opposite the Proline shop at Fountain. **Please call 9664127296** for appointments. So look in your mirror and tell yourself you've finally found the guy you'd like to spend the rest of your life with, and then call me and come on down. I'm waiting to meet you. Don't worry if you're nervous because I'm probably twice as nervous as you are ! I won't be in Mumbai for too long, so don't hesitate. See you soon.

Did you know that print subscribers to *Granta* also get access to over one hundred and thirty back issues on granta.com? That means . . .

Diana Athill **Margaret Atwood Iain Banks** Julian Barnes
Ned Beauman Fatima Bhutto Roberto Bolaño
Anne Carson Eleanor Catton **Noam Chomsky**
Bret Easton Ellis **James Ellroy Louise Erdrich**
Jonathan Franzen **Janine di Giovanni**
Nadine Gordimer Mark Haddon Seamus Heaney
A.M. Homes Nick Hornby **Kazuo Ishiguro A.L. Kennedy**
Stephen King **Nicole Krauss Doris Lessing**
Nelson Mandela **Hilary Mantel Ian McEwan**
David Mitchell Lorrie Moore Herta Müller **Alice Munro**
David Peace Mary Ruefle **Salman Rushdie**
Taiye Selasi **Will Self Gary Shteyngart** Zadie Smith
Rebecca Solnit **Andrea Stuart** Paul Theroux
John Updike Binyavanga Wainaina Joy Williams
and Jeanette Winterson

. . . to name a few.

Not a subscriber? Visit granta.com or complete the form overleaf.

GRANTA
THE MAGAZINE OF NEW WRITING

PRINT SUBSCRIPTION REPLY FORM FOR US, CANADA
AND LATIN AMERICA (includes digital access).
For digital-only subscriptions, please visit granta.com/subscriptions.

GUARANTEE: If I am ever dissatisfied with my *Granta* subscription, I will simply notify you, and you will send me a complete refund or credit my credit card, as applicable, for all un-mailed issues.

YOUR DETAILS

TITLE ....

NAME ....

ADDRESS ....

....

CITY... STATE ....

ZIP CODE .... COUNTRY...............................

EMAIL ....

☐ Please check this box if you do not wish to receive special offers from *Granta*

☐ Please check this box if you do not wish to receive offers from organisations
   selected by *Granta*

YOUR PAYMENT DETAILS

1 year subscription: ☐ US: $48   ☐ Canada: $56   ☐ Latin America: $68

3 year subscription: ☐ US: $120   ☐ Canada: $144   ☐ Latin America: $180

Enclosed is my check for $ _____ made payable to *Granta*.
Please charge my: ☐ Visa   ☐ MasterCard   ☐ Amex

Card No. ☐☐☐☐☐☐☐☐☐☐☐☐☐☐☐☐

Expiration date ☐☐ / ☐☐

Security Code ☐☐☐☐☐

SIGNATURE .... DATE ....

Please mail this order form with your payment instructions to:

Granta Publications
PO Box 359
Congers, NY 10920-0359

Or call 845-267-3031
Or visit GRANTA.COM/SUBSCRIPTIONS for details

Source code: BUS132PM

FREUD MUSEUM LONDON
Sigmund Freud's final home

Step into Sigmund Freud's London home and discover his intriguing study, his collection of antiquities and his famous psychoanalytic couch.

Open Wednesday to Sunday, 12 noon-5pm
Admission charge. ⊖Finchley Road

Summer Exhibition: *Festival of the Unconscious*
24 June - 4 October 2015

20 Maresfield Gardens, London NW3 5SX
+44 (0) 207 435 2002

www.freud.org.uk

Courtesy of the author

BANDIT

Molly Brodak

I

I was with my dad the first time I stole something: a little booklet of baby names. I was seven and I devoured word lists: dictionaries, vocab sheets, menus. The appeal of this string of names, their sweet weird shapes and neat order, felt impossible to solve. I couldn't ask for such a pointless thing but I couldn't leave it either. I pressed it to my chest as we walked out of Kroger. It was pale blue with the word BABY spelled out in pastel blocks above a stock photo of a smiling white baby in a white diaper. I stood next to Dad, absorbed in page one, as he put the bags of our food in the trunk of his crappy gold Chevette and he stopped when he saw it. At first he said nothing. He avoided my eyes. He just pressed hard into my back and marched me to the lane we'd left and plucked the stupid booklet out of my hand and presented it to the cashier.

'My daughter stole this. I apologize for her.' He beamed a righteous look over a sweep of people nearby. The droopy cashier winced and muttered that it was OK, chuckling mildly. Then, stooping over me, Dad shouted cleanly, 'Now you apologize. You will never do this again.' The cold anger in his face was edged with some kind of glint I didn't recognize. As he gripped my shoulders he was almost smiling.

I remember his shining eyes and the high ceiling of the gigantic store and the brightness of it. I am sure I cried but I don't remember. I do remember an acidic boiling in my chest and a rinse of sweaty cold on my skin, a disgust with my own desire and what it did, how awful all of us felt now because of me. I never stole again until I was a teenager, when he was in prison.

2

Dad robbed banks one summer.

He robbed the Community Choice Credit Union on 13 Mile Road in Warren.

He robbed the Warren Bank on 19 Mile Road.

He robbed the NBD Bank in Madison Heights.

He robbed the NBD Bank in Utica.

He robbed the TCF Bank on 10 Mile Road in Warren.

He robbed the TCF Bank on 14 Mile in Clawson. That was my bank. The one with the little baskets of Dum Dums at each window and sour herb smell from the health-food store next door.

He robbed the Credit Union One on 15 Mile Road in Sterling Heights.

He robbed the Michigan First Credit Union on Gratiot in Eastpointe.

He robbed the Comerica Bank on 8 Mile and Mound. This was as close as he got to the Detroit neighborhood he grew up in, Poletown East, about ten miles south.

He robbed the Comerica Bank inside of a Kroger on 12 Mile and Dequindre.

He robbed the Citizens State Bank on Hayes Road in Shelby Township. The cops caught up with him finally, at Tee J's Golf Course on 23 Mile Road. They peeked into his parked car: a bag of money and his disguise in the back seat, plain as day. He was sitting at the bar, drinking a beer and eating a hot ham sandwich.

3

I was thirteen that summer. He went to prison for seven years after a lengthy trial, delayed by constant objections and rounds of firing his public defenders. After his release he lived a normal life for seven years, and then robbed banks again.

There: see? Done with the facts already. The facts are easy to say; I say them all the time. This isn't about them. This is about whatever is cut from the frame of narrative. The fat remnants, broken bones, gristle, untender bits.

I'd sit at the dinner table watching my parents' volley crescendo from pissy fork drops to plate slams to stomp-offs and squeal-aways, my sister biting into the cruel talk just to feel included, me just watching as if on the living-room side of a television screen: I could see them but they could definitely not see me. I squashed my wet veggies around on my plate, eyes fixed to the drama like it was *Scooby-Doo* or *G.I. Joe*. I could sleep, I could squirm, I could hum, dance or even talk, safe in their blind spot. I could write, I discovered, and no one heard me.

4

Yes, one day it was like a membrane breached: before, Dad was like all other dads, and then he was not. We sat together at Big Boy, our booth flush against the winter-black windows reflecting back a weak pair of us, and I idly asked him what recording studios are like and how they work. I was something like eleven, and I had a cloudy notion that it would be exciting and romantic to work in a recording studio for some reason, to help create music but not have to play it. He fluttered his eyes upward like he did and answered without hesitation.

He told me about the equipment and how bands work with producers, how much sound engineers make and what their schedules are like. Details, I started to realize, he could not possibly know. Some giant drum began turning behind my eyes.

Very slowly, as he talked, I felt my belief, something I didn't really know was there until I felt it moving, turn away from him until it was gone, and I was alone, nodding and smiling. But what a marvel to watch him construct bullshit.

After that, I could always tell when he was lying. Something changed around his eyes when he spoke, a kind of haze or color shift, I could see it.

5

It's the day after Thanksgiving and I've forgotten to write to him. I log into the Federal Bureau of Prisons' email system, called CorrLinks, and check my inbox. No new messages from him in the past month. I try to find the last email exchange we had but it's all empty: the messages are only archived for thirty days, then they disappear.

I write to him like I'd write to a pen pal – distanced, a little uncertain, with a plain dullness I know is shaped by the self-conscious awareness that someone screens these messages before he reads them, even though their content is never more than polite and bloodlessly broad life updates.

How's the new job? Is it interesting? I ask. I remember he told me he upgraded from a job rolling silverware in the kitchen for $2 a day to a 'computer job' – previewing patent applications and rejecting them if incomplete. *I got a new cat. She's kind of shy but funny, with one white spot right on her chest. Her name's Jupiter.* I feel like I'm talking to a child. *Hope you are staying warm there!*

I eat lunch, grade papers, go for a walk, check back for a response, spurred by nagging and pointless guilt. No response. He's pushing seventy, with failing kidneys, and I sometimes wonder if he'll make it to his release date. Or even to another email.

The day passes. I try to forget about him. Then, I do forget about him. Days slip by, weeks.

Almost a month later I receive a Christmas card from his girlfriend. *Merry Christmas Molly – you're a doll!*

Below her signature is his, pressed on by a stamp she had made of it. Enclosed is a check for $300, also with his signature stamped on it.

6

In the window of the cab our beachfront hotel approached like a dream, as wrong as a dream, and I felt sick and overwhelmed with the luxury of the fantastic palm trees and clean arched doorways. This could not be right. As we left the cab I hung my mouth open a little long in joy and suspicion, for him to see. He made a roundabout pointing sweep to the door and said, 'Lezz go,' goofily, like he did. Thinking about it now, the hotel was probably nothing special, maybe even cheap, but I couldn't have known.

This was the longest period of time we spent alone together. I was nine or ten and he'd brought me to Cancún, an unlikely place to take a child for no particular reason. He had a habit of taking vacations with just me or my sister, never both of us together, and never with Mom, even when they were married. I feel there was a reason for this; the reason feels dark and I don't like to guess at it.

During the day he would leave me. I'd wake up and find a key and a note on top of some money: *Have fun! Wear sunscreen!* I'd put on my nubby yellow bathing suit and take myself to the beach or the small, intensely chlorinated pool and try hard to have a fun vacation, as instructed.

What was he doing? Was there somewhere nearby to gamble? There must have been. Or was there a woman he met? He'd return in the evening and take me to eat, always ordering a hamburger and a Coke for me without looking at the menu, even though I hated hamburgers and Coke. Mom wouldn't let me drink soda, and he liked to break this rule of hers.

'*Hahmm-borrr-gaysa*,' he'd say to the waiter, childishly drawing out the words and gesturing coarsely as if the waiter were near blind and deaf, 'and *Coca-Colé!*' he'd finish, pairing the silly 'olé!' with an insulting bottle-drinking mime. He was condescending to waiters everywhere, big-shot style, but especially here. 'This is the only word you need to know,' he told me from across the dark booth. '*Hamburguesa.*' I tamped down my disgust with obliging laughs, since this show was for me. His gold chain and ring I did not recognize. I watched him carefully, waiting for a time when we'd say real things to each other.

I didn't tell him I liked my days there, on the beach, alone like a grown-up. But anxious. I knew the untethered feeling I liked was not right for me yet. I would have told him about my days lying on a blue towel, just lying there for hours burning pink in the sun, listening while two teenage Mexican girls talked next to me, oblivious to my eavesdropping, alternating between Spanish and English. They talked about how wonderful it would be to be born a *gringa,* and what kind of house they'd live in and what their boyfriends would look like and how their daddies would spoil them with cars and clothes and fantastic birthday parties.

Once, he waited for me to wake up and took me to a Mayan ruin. As the tour started, the foreigners drew together automatically to climb the giant steep steps of a pyramid. It was soaking hot, and I felt so young and small. The other tourists seemed to have such trouble climbing. I bounded up the old blocks, turning to the wide mush of treetops below and smiling. Dad was down below. I waved to him but he wasn't looking. We were herded up for the tour and kids my age and even older were already whining. I couldn't imagine complaining even half as much as my peers did. It frightened me, the way they said what they wanted. *Hungry* and *tired* and *thirsty* and *bored* and *ugh, Dad, can we go*? At the edge of the cenote nearby a tour guide described how the Mayans would sacrifice young women here by tossing them in, 'girls about your age', he said, and pointed at me. The group of tourists around us chuckled uncomfortably but I straightened up.

I rested on a boulder carved into a snake's head, wearing the only hat I owned as a child, a black-and-neon tropical-print baseball cap I am certain came from a Wendy's kids' meal. I remember seeing a photograph taken of this, and I wonder if it still exists somewhere.

I remember resting on the snake's head, and I remember the photograph of myself resting on it. I liked this day, seeing these things that seemed so important, Dad mostly hanging back in the wet shade of the jungle edge, not climbing things. But he had brought me here and I loved it. I felt the secret urge children have to become lost and stay overnight somewhere good like a museum or a mall as a way of being there privately, directly. I circled the pyramid hoping to find a cave where I could curl up, so I could sleep and stay in this old magic and feel like I'd be a good sacrifice, just right for something serious. But it was hot and we had to go. Dad seemed tired, suspicious of it all, not especially interested in learning too much from the guide or in looking too hard at the ruins. I was happy, though, and he was pleased with that, seemed to want to let me have my happiness without necessarily caring to share in it or talk about it.

On the way back, the tour van we were in had to stop for gas. Children my age but much skinnier came to the windows with their hands out, pleading, keeping steady eye contact. Some tourists in the van gave them coins. The kids who received coins immediately pocketed them and stretched their hands out again, empty. I looked at my dad. He laughed dismissively. 'They're just bums. They can work like the rest of us.'

And then, back to the days like before, which now seemed even longer. I grew tired of the pretty beach. The tourists were loud, desperate in their drinking and their little radios. I sat alone in the hotel room. It was yellow and clean and there was a small TV I would flip through endlessly. *We are just not ... friends*, I remember thinking. I wondered who was friends with Dad. Mom? That seemed insane. My sister? Yes, her. She'd be good at this, being here with him. She'd be having the time of her life, sucking down a virgin strawberry daiquiri and posing poolside, hamming it up for Dad's camera. The hallways were tiled brown and cold, and the smell of chlorine from the pool seemed trapped forever in the corridors, night and day. I would walk around the hotel with the $20 bill he had given me for food, not sure what to do with it.

7

I want to say plainly everything I didn't know.

I didn't know Dad gambled. Sports betting mostly, on football, baseball or college basketball, point spreads, totals, money lines, whatever was offered. Bookies, calls to Vegas, two or three TVs at once.

I knew there were little paper slips and crazy phone calls and intense screaming about games – more intense than seemed appropriate – but it only added up to a kind of private tension orbiting him. I didn't know what it was.

Sports betting is so different from card games or other gambling because the player doesn't *play* the game, exactly. His game is the analysis of information – knowing which players might be secretly hurt or sick, which refs favor which teams, the mood of one stadium over another, the combination of one pitcher with a certain kind of weather – and the synthesis of hunches, superstitions, wishes, loyalty. And beyond that there are the odds the bookies are offering, which reflect what everyone else is predicting. Perfect for someone who thinks he's smarter than everyone else.

Before Detroit built big casinos downtown there was always Windsor Casino across the Canadian border, so there was always blackjack too. But nobody knows much about this – my mom, my sister, his co-workers, his brothers and sisters – no one saw his gambling, no one was invited to come along, or share strategy, or even wish him luck. It was totally private. Perhaps it would not have been so evil if it hadn't been so hidden. Mom's experience of his gambling came to her only in cold losses: an empty savings account, the car suddenly gone, bills and debts, threatening phone calls. Sometimes broken ribs, a broken nose. The rare big win must have been wasted immediately in private, on more gambling or something showy and useless like a new watch. Or, of course, on his debts.

Outcomes get shaken out fast in gambling. In real life, big risks take years to reveal themselves, and the pressure of choosing a career, a partner, a home, a family, a whole identity might overwhelm an impatient man, one who values control, not fate. He will either want all the options out of a confused greed, hoarding overlapping partners, shallow hobbies, alternate selves, or he will refuse them all, risking nothing. And really, the first option is the same as the second. Keeping a few girlfriends or wives around effectively dismisses a true relationship with any one of them. Being a good, hardworking dad and a criminal at the same time is a way of choosing to be neither.

Besides, an addict is already faithfully committed to something he prioritizes above all else. Gambling addiction, particularly, is easy to start; it requires no elaborate or illegal activities, no troublesome ingestion of substances and it programs the body using its own chemicals. I thought at first gambling was about chance, the possibility of making something out of nothing, of multiplying money through pure cleverness. He'd like that. Something from nothing. And that is the first charm. But the ones who get addicted, I think, are looking for certainty, not chance. Outcomes are certain, immediate and clear. In other words, there *will* be a result to any one bet, a point in time when the risk will be unequivocally resolved, and the skill and foresight of the gambler can be perfectly measured. A shot of adrenaline will issue into the bloodstream, win *or* lose. It's not messy, not indefinite or uncontrollable, like love, or people. Gambling absolves its players of uncertainty.

8

Dad steered Mom through the broad doors of the restaurant at the Hazel Park Raceway for their first date. The old host lit up, welcomed him by name and seated them by the wide windows. The waiters knew him too, and he tipped outrageously. Mom wore a baggy white hippie smock embroidered with lines of tiny red flowers (a dress, she said, like 'a loose interpretation of a baseball'), and her wild black curly hair down in a plain cloud. Dad wore a gold-button sports jacket, creased slacks, hard-shined shoes and slick hair; a near Robert

De Niro. They'd met while working in a tool and die shop in Romeo, Michigan, in 1977. Mom had been placed there for a few weeks by a temp agency to do packing and shipping.

After only a couple months of dating, Dad took her on an elaborate vacation to South America to see Machu Picchu. He'd first suggested Mexico, but Mom said she didn't like Mexico. It made her nervous.

The trip was impulsive and strange, something my mom would have loved. And he seemed so rich. He'd told her, I imagine in his shy way, without eye contact, that if he ever were to marry someone, it would be her. Mom felt adored, scooped up in his big gestures, bound by the certainty of them. I have seen some photographs from this trip. They both look so excited and free and wild, in jeans and thin T-shirts, laughing, almost childish against the ancient monuments and green vistas. He directed the trip with sheer confidence, ever-calm, bullying through the language barrier, tossing indulgences to my mom along the way like the king of the parade. She didn't know he had cashed out a life insurance policy to take her there, and that he was dead broke. Soon after the trip she discovered she was pregnant with my sister.

Mom's pregnancy started to show at the shop, drawing stronger looks from the bitter receptionist with the beehive hairdo. Mom noticed the looks, and turned to her, straight and direct, like she always did if something needed to be sorted out.

'Darlin'', the receptionist said before Mom even opened her mouth, 'he didn't tell you he's married, did he?'

Mom laughed but said nothing. The receptionist just shook her head in pity. Mom didn't like pity. She would have ignored it. He had told her he'd marry her if he was ever inclined to marry, and it just didn't seem to her like something someone already married could come up with. It was so sweet. He was *so* generous, so affectionate.

The idea, though, began to itch. She did think it was odd that she had never been to his house, didn't have his home phone number and had only been offered vague indications of where he lived. That night she asked him if he was married, and he said no. He acted genuinely confused, suggesting that the receptionist was just a jealous cow because he wouldn't flirt with her. She felt happy with that. And besides, there was a baby to consider now. She let it go. Soon, she moved into an apartment with him and quit working.

For her first doctor's visit, Dad gave her his insurance card and the name of the clinic to visit while he was at work. She handed over the card to the receptionist, who pulled a file, opened it and then paused. The receptionist looked at Mom, then at the file, then at Mom again, glancing at the nurses near her to spread her discomfort. An indignant look hardened her face. Mom was puzzled. 'Is everything OK?' she finally asked.

'Yes, but . . . I'm sorry, ma'am . . . but you are not Mrs Brodak.'

Mom smiled politely. 'Well, not officially yet, but I'm on his insurance now so you have to honor that.'

'No, I mean . . .' The nurses now looked on with worry. 'Mrs Brodak and her daughter are regular patients of this clinic. They were just in last Wednesday. *You* are not Mrs Brodak.'

It was then, she told me, that it should have ended. It wasn't too late. 'Everything,' she told me, 'could have been avoided if I had just gone back to my parents instead of to him the moment I left that clinic.' I nod, imagining how much better that would have been for her, skipping past the idea that this 'everything' she could have avoided would have included me. 'It's like all I could do was make mistakes,' she said.

The moment he stepped through the door that evening she told him the story of the insurance card at the clinic and demanded to know who the real Mrs Brodak was. He softened his shoulders and toddled gently to her, engulfing her with a hug, caressing her as she cried. His softness and confident denial stunned her into silence, just like it had before. He told her the woman was just a friend he'd allowed to use his card, that he was just doing someone a favor out of kindness, that he was certainly not married. He laughed about it, prodding and rousing her into laughing with him as he smoothed her face.

He could turn you like that. He just wouldn't let your bad mood win. He'd steal your mad words and twist them funny in repetition, poke at your folded arms until they opened, grin mockingly at your dumb pout until you smiled, as long as it took.

A few days later she called the county clerk's office to inquire about some marriage records. The clerk on the other end delivered the news plainly, as she probably always did. He'd been married for just a few years. He had a daughter, aged four.

See, this is how my dad starts – stolen from another family.

Mom packed her small suitcases and moved to her parents' house that same day, and that, again, should've been the end of it. She stayed in her room. The road to her parents' house had not been paved yet, and there were still fields around them, overgrown lilac bushes, honeysuckle and wild rhubarb where now there are neighbors' neat lawns.

She thought about his tenderness. The honest, steady light in his eyes when he told her he loved her. How he'd suddenly sweep her up for a small dance around the kitchen. All these things he'd practiced with his real wife. She gave birth to my sister, quietly.

But he wouldn't leave her alone. He found her and would come whenever he could, tossing rocks at her window in the night like a teenager until her father chased him off, leaving bouquets on the doorstep with long love letters. He was unreasonably persistent, beyond what she would've expected of any boyfriend, and perhaps it was the insane magnitude of this persistence that convinced her to go back to him. She thought maybe their relationship was worth all of this effort, all of the dozens and dozens of roses, the gifts, the jewelry, the long letters pleading for forgiveness, praising her virtues, promising to leave his wife. 'And poetry,' Mom said. 'You should have seen the poetry he wrote to me. I almost wish I hadn't thrown it all away.'

First she wanted to meet the real Mrs Brodak. Mom looked up their number in the phone book, called to introduce herself and extend an invitation to meet, which Mrs Brodak accepted stiffly.

It was a muggy summer. Dad's wife appeared at the screen door and stood without knocking. In a thick blue dress with her waist tied tightly, she said nothing when Mom opened the door. 'Would you like to hold the baby?' Mom asked.

My sister was placed in her lap like a bomb. Nothing could be done but politely talk, with hard grief in their chests, softening their voices. The real Mrs Brodak was scared too. 'How did you meet?' Mom asked Dad's wife.

They had met in high school. After he had returned from Vietnam, they married impulsively. She never had time to think, she said. Baby, work, no time to think. This is how life works: hurrying along through the tough moments, then the hurrying hardens and fossilizes, then that's the past, that hurrying. She asked Mom what was going to happen now.

'Now,' Mom said, 'we leave Joe Brodak. We don't let our babies know him. He's not a good person.' She leaned to her, with hands out. They lightly embraced and nodded tearfully. Mom would have wanted to help Mrs Brodak.

Mom also would have felt a little triumphant somehow. She would have felt like she had won him. Whatever there was to win. She didn't actually want to quit like that, despite what she said to Mrs Brodak. She had a baby now, and no real career prospects, having ditched the student teaching she needed to finish her certification, and on top of that her own mental illnesses kept her from self-sufficiency. Her parents looked on with reserved worry. After Dad's wife left, Mom joined them in the kitchen, where they had been listening to the exchange. They sipped coffee, looking out at the bird feeder. Eventually Mom's mother urged her to go back to him. 'It is better to be married,' she said. 'You have to just deal with it.'

She turned back to him, resolved to trust him.

This looks bad, I know. I would not have made this choice, I think. Most people wouldn't. But what do any of us know?

In the basement of the Romeo District Court my dad married my mom, with his sister, Helena, as a witness. The dress Mom wore, an off-white peasant dress with low shoulders and small pouf sleeves, I wore when I was ten, as a hippie Halloween costume.

A small dinner party was held at a restaurant on a nearby golf course. Mom met her mother-in-law there, and many other Brodaks, who all regarded her warily. As a homewrecker.

Soon after the wedding, I was born, during a year of relative happiness in their relationship. Perhaps, Mom thought, their rocky start was over, that there would be no more problems. She threw her wild energy into this life: these children, and him, *her* husband, now. She enacted a vigorous and healthy routine for her family: reading, games, walks to the park, dancing, art and helping the elderly lady upstairs with her housework. She attended to us with pure devotion. She baked homemade bread and wrote folk songs, singing them softly to us with her acoustic Gibson at bedtime. The songs were always minor key, lament-low, about horses and freedom and the ocean. In the dark, I'd cry sometimes in their hold.

Mom isn't sure exactly when Dad got divorced from his first wife; he kept the details a secret. With her daughter, my half-sister, Mrs Brodak moved to California, where she died of cancer a few years later.

9

Mom threw away all of the letters and poetry he'd sent her when she remarried and moved in with her new husband. It stings to think about. I wish I could have read these things, but they were not for me. And I don't blame her.

But I did see the letters, a long time ago. I saw the shoebox full of them when I was little. Pages and pages of blue-lined notebook paper with Dad's loopy, fat, cursive writing, or sometimes the harsh, slanted caps he'd use. The words rattled on the pages with some mysterious grown-up intensity that pushed me away from them. I did take something from the box. A thing that made no sense to me.

A small, square, black-and-white photo of him he had sent her.

The background is pure white and the whiteness of his knit polo shirt disappears into it so his head appears to be floating in whiteness, rooted only by the wide, heathered gray collar of his shirt. He is young and smiling broadly, open-mouthed, joy in his eyes, like he was just laughing, really laughing. He's smiling honestly, more honestly than I have ever seen.

On the back of the photo is his loopy cursive in blue pen. When I read it I began to cry instantly, in gusting sheets of tears. I took it because it was the first object that made me cry. I couldn't understand how. I'm crying now, reading it again.

Nora,

My first real, true love. You changed my life with your 'crazy' love.

I love you,

J.B.

10

After I was born Dad came across an ad for an attorney who was hiring women to be surrogate mothers. He became convinced that this would solve their financial problems. Nowadays paid surrogacy is common, but in the early eighties the process was new, and still somewhat risky. He pressed my mother, and she started to warm to the idea; after all, she loved being a mother and felt good about the idea of helping a couple have a baby. It seemed kind and smart and wonderful. She said the couple met her in a restaurant, and she brought me and my sister along, 'you know, to show you off, so they could see how healthy and happy you were', she told me. We squirmed and smiled in the booth like the best roly-poly babies possible, and Mom beamed while the couple fell for her.

They lived in Long Island, so Mom was flown out to New York to do the insemination there. It didn't work. She was flown out again. It didn't work.

Meanwhile, Dad's gambling debts were secretly starting to accumulate. He was thinking about the $10,000 they were set to receive as soon as the baby was born, and had started spending recklessly. Mom started noticing odd things. Some men had asked the neighbors where the Brodak girls went to school. The phone rang off the hook. Only once did she respond, finding a strange man on the line. He told her he was calling from Vegas. 'Your husband,' the man said, 'is a scumbag. A fucking deadbeat. Did you know that?' She unplugged the phone. That night, the living-room windows were shot out.

Dad told her they needed to move. And why not to Long Island, to be closer to the couple? To him it was the perfect out.

We moved to a cramped basement apartment on Long Island. In photos of us from this era, on a cheap swing set or feeding ducks by a weak pond, there is a kind of stressy child anger in our eyes. Mom kept up her focus on us. Free from his debts back in Michigan, Dad returned to gambling. She never knew how bad things were until something went missing.

Mom was cleaning us up from breakfast one day when Dad was leaving for work. He came back through the door after a minute. 'Forget something?' Mom asked absently.

'No, uh, my car . . .'

Mom looked out the window. It was gone, had disappeared overnight. 'Where's your car?'

'Oh . . . I let a buddy of mine borrow it.'

'He just came in the night and took your car? He had a key to your car?'

'Yeah, it was an emergency, no big deal. I'm gonna borrow yours today, OK?' He grabbed her keys and left.

How could he resolve this one? Weeks went by and his 'buddy' didn't return the car. Eventually he just came home with a new one, an old beater with green upholstery smelling of dogs. He told Mom he'd decided to sell his buddy the car, but she'd already seen the repo notice. She wasn't surprised anymore. She shuffled her rage into resignation, and focused on us.

The insemination attempts continued. One night, after returning from a long trip, drunk and tired, Dad forced himself on her. Mom said she screamed and fought him. But he was strong. Sex was against the contract they had with the couple, for obvious reasons.

On a hunch, she took a test a few weeks later and discovered she was pregnant. Now, though, she wasn't sure whose baby it was.

She took us to stay with her aunt in Baltimore for a few weeks. And there, without telling anyone, she decided to abort the fetus. She hadn't spoken to Dad for weeks, nor did she return the calls from the couple. Eventually she returned home, with us in tow, to find Dad having just returned too, from Atlantic City. He had gambled away everything. Their savings, his car, his wedding ring, every penny he could find. She packed our clothes and whatever small things would fit into her powder-blue Caprice Classic and took us back to Michigan that same day. She filed for divorce and moved back in with her parents. It was here, living with my grandparents, that I first started to know my life. I remember Goodison Preschool. A salt-dough Christmas ornament I made and tried to eat. Playing Red Rover in the sun. My bossy sister teasing me, and stress around us all.

Eventually she was going to have to call the couple to tell them what happened. She says she still remembers that phone call, their voices on the other line, warm, but quiet and shocked. They were crushed. They said they would have taken the baby either way, and loved it completely. They had come to trust and care for her, and she failed them in the worst possible way. Listening to my mom reveal this story crumples me inside.

She was about my age when this happened, and I imagine her next to me, as a friend. I would have helped her out of this.

I would have shaken her bony shoulders and said *no no no no* until the stupid false hope in her eyes was gone and all of Dad's tricks fell away.

11

Such a short part of their lives, really, this marriage and this family. Just a few years.

Dad moved back to Michigan too, following us a few weeks later. He was living in a hotel room in Center Line, near the GM Tech Center where he worked.

We'd be dropped off there, and walk the AstroTurf-lined walkways to the room while teenagers screamed and splashed in the pool. Mexican music blared and faded in the rooms we passed, some with open doors, some with eyes following. But it was a break from the attentive care children can get sick of. It seemed like a party. He bought us huge bags of candy – Skittles for my sister and Raisinets for me. There were always cold cuts and a shrimp ring in the fridge. During the day he'd often leave us alone, and we were OK, watching movies, eating candy, puffy-painting giant cheap sweatshirts and playing Nintendo. I didn't really miss him when he was gone, and I knew that couldn't be right.

My sister took care of me when we were alone. She directed me to eat the crackers and ham she'd arranged and have a glass of milk while I was absorbed in *Mega Man*. She knew how to pull out the sofa bed when we were getting tired. I'd watch her tiny body rip the creaky metal frame out of the nubby brown couch. She'd straighten the sheets around the lumpy mattress and drag the comforter from Dad's bed onto ours, nestling me into the uncomfortable mess wordlessly.

She'd check to make sure the door was deadbolted, then flip the lights off and tuck us in. The puffy paints and bags of candy and the half-consumed glasses of milk and the ham plates would be scattered on the floor around the sofa bed, and we'd just lie there, listening. The rush of 12 Mile Road below and the garbled living sounds from the other residents would lull us to sleep. We imagined different versions of where Dad was. A cool movie, on a date with a hot lady, at a nightclub, at a concert. Sometimes we'd compare ideas, sometimes we'd just let them play out in our heads as we fell asleep.

During the day I'd poke around his stuff. Shoved under towels in the linen closet: *Playboys* and baggies of green and white drugs. Sometimes money. Under the bed, in a shoebox: a heavy, greasy-looking gun.

I wanted to have the fun he wanted us to have. He'd take us to things, kid things, like water parks or Chuck E. Cheese's, places Mom would never take us because she insisted on productive activities like hikes or art museums. He'd take us to a golf dome with a bar and a dark arcade attached, then hand us both a roll of quarters to spend in the arcade while he was in the bar. For hours we'd feed the machines, Mortal Kombat and Rampage and Gauntlet. When our quarters were gone we'd gingerly shuffle through the bar and find him alone, glued to a sports game. He'd hand us more quarters or say it was time to go. It was fun but, I don't know, thin fun. He'd put something in front of us: a sports game or play place or movie or toy and he was always on the other side of it, far on the other side of it. I kept it that way too, I know. I didn't like to go with him, I didn't like to have to answer his perfunctory questions about school or interests, I didn't even like to hug him. I feel awful remembering this.

And, once again, he pursued Mom relentlessly, but I never saw it happen and didn't know this until later, when Mom told me. I often wonder why he did it. He could have easily walked away from us, and perhaps he didn't only because that was the more obvious thing to do. The only thing that makes sense is that he wanted to be with us. Or that he felt like he was supposed to be with us, an obligation he couldn't shake.

I should be able to feel my way through that question, to be able to know, in my gut, if he really wanted to be a dad and husband. But I can't feel it. Nothing really matches up. There are fragments of a criminal alongside fragments of a dad, and nothing overlaps, nothing eclipses the other, they're just there, next to each other. No narrative fits.

12

No, I did see it, once. On a softball field in the evening when the sky was getting dark pink. Mom had brought me to see my sister's softball team play, a team that my dad coached. I had wandered away to sit in the grass, probably looking for interesting insects or rocks, and from some distance I saw my dad approach my mom at the edge of the bleachers where she stood. The sun was behind them but I could see their gray shapes in the nook of the gleaming silver bleachers and the matching fence. Perhaps the game was over. He was talking closely to her face and she was looking away at first, arms crossed. I edged to the other side of the bleachers to hear. He had his hand on her shoulder; she was starting to smile. I could hear him say, 'I need you. I need you,' in a steady pleading voice I can still hear in my head. I was surprised at this sound, and memorized it. Then he lifted his knee and softly and childishly kneed her thigh, still saying, 'I need you' and now drawing it out lightly and funnily with each jab – 'I *kneed* you. I *kneed* you,' – and she was really smiling now, looking down sweetly and smiling.

13

My dad was born August 19, 1945, in a displaced persons' camp. This is how he first lived: being carried by his mother, in secret, while she worked silently in the camp.

The previous year his mother and father and five siblings had been moved out of their homes in Szwajcaria, Poland, by the Nazis and forced to board a train. My Aunt Helena, a few years older than my dad, told me she remembers it. She remembers their mom, Stanislawa, hopping off the train when it stopped to hunt for wood to start a cooking fire. Stanislawa's parents and three of her siblings had died a few years before in Siberia, having been shipped there to cut trees for the Russian supply. 'The trees would shatter if they hit the ground because it was so cold. No one had enough clothes or food, so most people died there,' my aunt told me in a letter. She has memories of their life during the war, 'but they don't seem real', she wrote. She remembers the mood of the train: the animal-like panic any time the train stopped, the worry of the adults, and her worry when her mother would disappear. They were taken to Dachau, where my grandfather was beaten and interrogated daily because the Nazis suspected him of being a partisan, like his brothers.

My grandfather was separated from the family. The rest of them lived and worked together, hoping he'd be returned. Nothing useful came out of the interrogations.

After a few months they were reunited, and all transferred to a sub-camp in Kempten, Germany, where they worked as slaves, mostly farming. This is where my grandmother became pregnant with my father. She hid her pregnancy because she was afraid she'd be forced to abort it. She had to work to be fed like everyone else, even the children, the sick, everyone. My aunt remembers a little of this but won't say much. 'There were horrors every day,' she says, and I don't press her. The war was over in April and my dad was born in August.

After the war, my grandfather felt strongly that they should move to Australia, since he liked the idea of working a homestead and living freely as a farmer. But a few months before they were to leave, he died, and Australia no longer welcomed them – a widow with five children. Through a Catholic sponsorship program a passage to America was offered, and they took it. My dad's first memories were of this ship: troop transport, cold and gray all around, the sea and metal smell.

14

They arrived at Ellis Island on December 4, 1951, and Dad's name was changed from Jozef to Joseph. They took a train to Detroit. Their sponsor took them to St Albertus Church, on the corner of St Aubin and Canfield, an area that used to be called Poletown. They lived on the top floor of the adjacent school, built in 1916, until my grandma found work in the cafeteria of the *Detroit News* and rented an apartment for them. St Albertus closed as a parish in 1990, and now stands in urban prairie among other abandoned buildings.

I wanted to see it for myself. One family visit in December I snuck away for the day and drove myself there. There are a lot of death holes in Detroit. Not poor neighborhoods but something beyond that: nothingnesses, forsaken places. Scattered plots, some whole blocks, whole streets, sets of streets, in the middle of the city. The place where my dad grew up is dead.

This area, around Mack and Chene, is one of the emptiest in Detroit. It is not the most dangerous; there just aren't many people here at all. Only a few structures stand on each block, and rarely are those structures occupied. Sometimes you can't really tell. Most houses are in different states of decay, some just piles of charred wood and ash. These are not the most picturesque ruins. They're not the famous ones, like the Packard Plant or the huge train depot, or the ornately ruined Michigan Theater. They're not the pretty castles of Brush Park, derelict and looted, the cool tall office buildings downtown with wild trees growing on them, the broken buildings out-of-town journalists and photographers come to document and vaguely lament. These were plain poor houses to start with.

St Albertus sits next to homes like these, and plots of empty grassland. Across the street is one occupied house, and a heavily gated new-but-cheap apartment complex, where a convent and girls' orphanage used to be. Behind the church is the school, a sturdy three-story brick building with a stone facade, ST ALBERTVS carved across a neoclassical frieze above four faceted pilasters between the doors. The school is a ruin – windows are broken or boarded up, graffiti covers the building man-high around the dark brick and the yard is grown over, with dumped TVs and furniture in the grass. I looked at it for a long time. This is where my family first lived in America. This is where my dad learned English. A ruin, like any other. I watched a solidly fat black squirrel climb the brick effortlessly, pause to eat a small thing on the windowsill, then disappear inside.

On the front steps I pulled shyly at the boards over the three doors, but they were nailed tight. It would have been easy enough to climb up to any of the glassless first-floor windows, but I was alone and it seemed unwise. I took some photos with my phone. A rind of green copper wound weakly around the roof, the rest of it having been pulled off by scavengers. I had explored abandoned structures before, but not alone. Still, here I was. I had come this far. I looked up and down the street, but there was not a soul around. I walked quickly to an inner corner and hoisted myself up on the ledge, then to the same glassless window into which the black squirrel had disappeared.

Broken glass and soft piles of crumbled plaster. Cold dark. The smell of old wet wood and dead animals. I dropped down into a classroom with gritty gray floors. But there had been some maintenance here by Church people; I could tell the floor had been swept occasionally. I walked like I was stepping on someone. The boards shivered and a steady wind hushed me.

A dark wood door lead to the hall, lined with more classrooms. All of the doorknobs removed, stolen. The next room was painted a sweet sky blue, peeling at the top, with a chalkboard but no furniture. A red fire-alarm box. Very nice wood, rotting. Powdery plaster making the ground soft. Every surface peeling. The next room was pale acid green. A patch of exposed cinder blocks where the chalkboard had been. It's hard to imagine my father as a boy. He was a star athlete, he'd told me. Captain of the football team in high school. He would've been fun. Quiet but brave and strong, like me. I kicked lightly at some planks on the ground, and the sound of scurrying claws in the walls moved away from me.

I went slowly down the hall, feeling ridiculous for using the flashlight feature on my expensive phone but glad to have it, since the floorboards were warped, with odd piles of glass and nails and wood shards. The bare rooms felt heavy and full, and I can't explain this. I came to a stairwell. Plaster dust had been swept into loose mounds against the wall, and footprints marked a path up the steps.

On the top floor, the hall opened into the auditorium. The windows were not boarded up here, and the room was bright and open and cold. I stood astounded: at one end a gaping black stage was framed with pale peach and jaunty blue leaf patterns, deco style, and flanked by two doors topped with Greek urns and vines of plaster. A very small gold-fringed pale blue curtain hung straight across the stage, painted with mounds of red and orange flowers with wispy grass behind.

My mouth hung dumbly and I started to cry. The peeling colors and the light of the room, the flowered curtain and the darkness, the piles of powder, the good wood, the hidden air. It was beautiful in a way I recognized in the oldest part of me. I felt like I was seeing something true. I walked the thin boards of the floor to the center of the room, past a large blue A painted inside of a circle, like a tidy anarchy symbol. Bird shit covered the floor, concentrating under grates. The cooing and wheezing and clawing of pigeons echoed blindly. Above the center of the room, on the high ceiling arching like a coffin top, was a trinity of large pale blue medallions, the center one probably once surrounding a light fixture that was now gone. My family slept on cots in this room for months. They looked up at this. As a child, my dad, packed in with the other refugees, looked up at this ceiling and thought about the future, this future I am in now. It was hard not to feel grateful for this useless beauty. It was there for them, this silent, mindless pattern, how it looked like love over the empty room.

The sky can be so solid gray in Michigan, like wet concrete, churning without breaking for days. Under it, this home, sinking into the earth, the earth digesting its own paradox, in silence. ∎

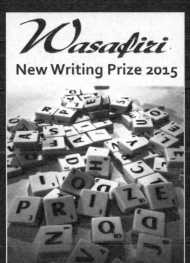

woman is a construct

woman is a construct
she must be

woman is basically meant
to be a residential complex
all the same
all plastered over
just in different colors

i in particular am a woman
with exposed bricks
at social gatherings i tend to be
the worst dressed

i say i'm a journalist

(woman is a construct
full of holes

leaking

cosmo is the ministry
of trash talk
excuse me
they don't write about shit in cosmo)

you are a woman
what if you suddenly wake up binary and blue
and spend all day turning the lights on and off?
(do you like being a brazilian woman?
do you like calling yourself virginia woolf?)

woman is a construct
makeup is camouflage

every woman has a gay friend
it's nice to have friends

all her friends have a gay friend
who has a wife
who calls him fred astaire

it's too late to change this
the psychologists at cafe freud
look at each other and laugh

nothing will change –

nothing will ever change –

woman is a construct

Translated from the Portuguese by Hilary Kaplan

Sadhana, 2012

THE BUDDHIST

Alan Rossi

While waiting for the sickness to pass, the Buddhist was not shirking his dharma-related responsibilities, was not skipping meditation, was not failing to practice in each and every moment, and was now, his laptop resting on his knees, getting ready to have a meeting with a student over Skype. He sat in the air-conditioned meditation hall, which was in the center of a Sri Lankan rainforest, waiting to connect with a student named Elise Grantwell, whom he had been teaching for the past six months.

It was the end of the rainy season. Outside the hall everything was darkly wet and green. The sun was not up yet. It was the time between night and morning where the sky went from a lightened gray to an impossibly clear blue. Out one window of the hall, the Buddhist could see Ajahn meditating with two other monks near the stream in the forest. They sat on bamboo mats. Because they all wore the saffron robes that were both customary and required of all monks in the Theravada Forest Tradition, they stood out against the backdrop of green forest. The monks, seated in variations of meditation posture by the river, were still, and the forest appeared to be moving, swirling around them. The Buddhist knew that the visual illusion was caused by his fever, yet he could not stop looking, fixated and momentarily light-headed, feeling vaguely disembodied, aware of the beauty of the scene and of the fact that he would soon not be in Sri Lanka and might never be there again, if that was Ajahn's wish. Then he inwardly chanted 'seeing, seeing' – knowing that his sense perception was ultimately devoid of self. The Buddhist thought of Ajahn's order to return to his home country, Canada, to help open a new temple there, and how he'd have to stay in the basement of his father's house, which had been his old room, now a little putting green thing. He tried to see his aversion to the notion of returning home for what it was: impermanent thinking of no reality, suffering that originated in ignorance and was caused by selfish craving, the craving in this case, he saw clearly, his own desire not to be where he would have to be, back in his home country. Staying on the AstroTurf floor of his father's basement – a man who tried to convey how much he disliked the Buddhist by not talking, choosing only to write him notes on Post-its even while the Buddhist was in his presence – was one of the only things the Buddhist believed he dreaded, even more than dying.

A request to connect through Skype blinked on the Buddhist's screen. He sat for a moment, hands composed in his lap on the saffron robes, and let his thoughts of sickness and returning home settle and calm, becoming clear, like dirt settling in water. He connected through Skype with Elise Grantwell. She was fortyish, lived in Washington DC and was – as she had explained to the Buddhist in an earlier email – having some intense episodes of stress, paranoia and self-loathing, which often led to panic attacks, all due to her job as a defense attorney. Her face appeared pixelated and slightly fuzzy on the Buddhist's screen. The image strained the Buddhist's fevered and tired eyes, which in turn made for an annoyed mind-state, though he told himself that such an annoyance was merely the discomfort of a certain sense perception, and that discomfort was only the consciousness of a certain physical ailment, namely the pain behind his fevered eyes, and also that it was a discomfort that would pass from his consciousness when the sickness passed from his body, which also meant – the fact that it would pass – that it contained no inherent reality, was not his self, and therefore it was nothing to dislike. It was, like all things, changing.

He tried to focus on Elise Grantwell's face. Elise Grantwell was white, had forty-year-old hair, just slightly thinning dark hair, and her face, almost pretty, seemed pulled down by gravity into a near-perpetual frown of seriousness or worry. She appeared to be wearing a pantsuit of some kind. The Buddhist noted that he felt a slight attraction to her over-worried yet almost pretty face, allowing the moment of sexuality to pass and fade.

The Buddhist told Elise Grantwell that he had read her email and was there anything else she wanted to add, any other questions? Elise Grantwell said yes, emphatically, on the Buddhist's screen. She said that since discovering Buddhism, which was at first very calming and stress-relieving, she felt even worse, because it (the meditation, the Buddhist presumed) had made her realize that her job – her life's work, she called it – could be considered something that prolonged or encouraged suffering rather than ending it. On the screen, Elise Grantwell appeared almost puzzle-like for a moment, the screen pixelating her face distressingly. So it's like the thing that was previously relieving my stress, she continued, her face blocky and blurred, the meditation itself and the teachings of dharma, you know, that's making my stress levels worse and causing me to have even more panic attacks. Her face resolved clearly on the Buddhist's screen. My stress is out of control, Elise Grantwell said.

He watched Elise Grantwell, whose eyes were mainly looking down, look very briefly up at the Buddhist then quickly back down again, nervy and submissive as a frightened animal. The Buddhist observed himself in the small boxy corner in the Skype window: visibly sweating and pale, yet composed. He tried not to scratch any part of the rash that had spread all over his body, and closed his eyes briefly. He inwardly labeled the sensation 'itchy, itchy', seeing that the reality of the sensation was no-self, filled with suffering, and impermanent. The feeling was not him – his body was the jug and his self was no self at all, just the emptiness inside.

Outside, the Sri Lankan morning was coming through the woods, the deep green of the forest revealing itself. The monks had completed seated meditation and the Buddhist could see, further into the forest, that they were walking on the path, doing walking meditation, looking a little like confused old men.

What if I got someone off who was guilty? Elise Grantwell wanted to know. Wasn't that somehow not Buddhist? Also, she said to the Buddhist, what if instead of making me less stressed and suffering *less*, I'm actually more stressed and suffering *more*? What if all this Buddhism stuff is bad for me? I'm just in a really bad place, she said, her brow furrowed in anxiety and confusion and her mouth tight. And meditation doesn't seem to be working *at all*, she said.

The Buddhist calmly nodded at his screen, watching Elise Grantwell's response and himself as he calmly nodded. He didn't engage with the fever behind his eyes, nor the intense itchiness of his body and, watching himself, he noticed he was exaggerating his nod so that if the connection was bad and/or briefly timed out, Elise Grantwell would still be able to see he was nodding and understanding. Elise Grantwell explained that it was not only that she was suffering more now *privately*; all this meditation seemed to be making her worse off around *other people* as well. All this calmness I'm trying to do is making people around me ask if I'm awake, she said. Like people are saying, *Hey, Elise, you awake over there?*, she said, both laughing and almost crying on his screen. The Buddhist observed himself listening, remaining calm, neutral, accepting. I'm just trying to calmly accept and be in difficult situations, like you've taught me, she explained to the Buddhist. But it's hard to be with angry and obnoxious colleagues in a meeting. It all seems to be making things *worse*, especially around other people, she told the Buddhist. And that's making me feel *so* alone and isolated, even *more* alone than before.

The Buddhist took a small breath. He observed himself in the corner of the screen sitting composedly in his saffron robes in lotus posture before his laptop, contemplating Elise Grantwell's situation and her being, acknowledging, with a small amount of pride, that he both felt and appeared earnest and attentive. Outside, the Sri Lankan rainforest was suddenly bright green and hummingly alive, insects making mechanical whirrings, as though someone had flipped a switch. The forest was a stark contrast to both his sickness and Elise Grantwell's sense of personal suffering in a materialistic and consumer-oriented culture, the Buddhist thought. He said to Elise Grantwell that he was deeply aware of how interpersonal relationships could quickly deteriorate once you took the first step on the path. He coughed and paused, momentarily feeling nauseated, a wave-like shuddering moving through his body. He allowed his presence to return to Elise Grantwell. The moment of nausea passed. The Buddhist said that Elise Grantwell's questions about other people and feeling alone were very apt. He was speaking calmly and directly and without hesitation, he thought, like a gentle rain addressing the sullen and dry earth.

For instance, the Buddhist said, these questions are very apt for me personally because I'll soon return to my home country, where I've had many difficult relationships, just as you are experiencing now. The idea of this other country where he had once lived, on the other side of the planet, momentarily passed through the Buddhist's mind, the country like some foreign world, and this idea instantly encompassed the place he was in now so that the Buddhist felt that all of existence, even himself, was foreign, alien, that everything was both alien unto itself and at the same time discovering itself to be completely and wholly unalien. The thought, more an intuitively felt experience of reality, passed so quickly that the Buddhist could easily continue what he was talking about. He explained to Elise Grantwell that his own interpersonal relationships had quickly deteriorated when he had been ordained as a Buddhist monk. While this didn't bother the Buddhist in the least now, it was also rather interesting for the truths it revealed about human behavior and how unaccepting almost all people who lived in a materialistic society were of a person who was no longer going to participate in the delusion of such a society. The immediate effects of such a change for him – of becoming a person who was calm, quiet, not unaffected but disaffected, not distant but detached – the Buddhist explained to Elise Grantwell, was that the people who had known him before intensive meditation and Buddhist study now believed him to be zombified, brainwashed, deadened. Asleep, the Buddhist shared openly with Elise Grantwell, who was nodding vigorously on the screen and saying Yes, yes.

When I first came home from Sri Lanka after ordaining, the Buddhist told her, after years of studying Buddhism, when I first returned to see family and friends, many people thought that I was asleep. The same thing people are thinking about you. Elise Grantwell was nodding earnestly, her eyes wide as a child's. Why wasn't I interested in climbing or kayaking anymore; why didn't I care about playing any of the instruments I used to play? I didn't joke the way I used to; I didn't drink, didn't do drugs or even seem to enjoy eating – everyone was basically saying the same thing. The Buddhist said that it was a strange irony that when one comes to see clearly that the three characteristics permeate all things – that all things have no separate self, all things are suffering and all things are impermanent, and that the only way to approach reality is through calm detachment and insight into this – the people who are actually asleep often accuse those who are really beginning to see of being asleep. Elise Grantwell said that that was just what she was thinking. My mother even went so far as to say I was brainwashed by a cult and wasting my life, the Buddhist told Elise Grantwell. I had to remind my mother that she hadn't approved of any of the activities like rock climbing and music that I'd done before anyway. I remember she said that anything would be better than what I'd chosen. Elise Grantwell nodded in the Skype window. The light darkened in the room, and he saw himself in the square of screen appearing thin and sickly and weak, yet composed. The Buddhist told Elise Grantwell that these were definitely deeply painful things and that he remembered them as being deeply painful and isolating. Yes, Elise Grantwell said. It's a little odd that this way also makes one understand one is alone, the Buddhist said. You're right that that first realization – that one is actually more alone than before, or can see one's aloneness with more clarity – you're right that that's painful. But it's a pain that passes, the Buddhist said.

The abbot came into the meditation hall and asked the Buddhist in Thai how his fever was. The abbot was a very old, very bald and very short Thai man who had a perpetual scowl on his face. His skin was brown, his face wrinkled. He was missing one of his front teeth and wore large, dark-framed glasses, which obscured his face and, the Buddhist believed, hid much of what he perceived of people. He spoke and responded to everything slowly, as inscrutable as an old dog. The Buddhist said he was feeling worse, but he knew it would pass. The abbot said, That's it! Which was what he said often and was his main dharma lesson, as though the entire world could be reduced to: This, It, Here, Now! The abbot, slightly bow-legged, went out again to look for the cook and said that he would try to round up breakfast. Outside, the high insect whine and buzz of the morning had intensified.

Sorry, the Buddhist said to Elise Grantwell, turning back to his screen. The Buddhist said that while he did remember being shunned, by his mother and, more spitefully, his father, as deeply painful and isolating, he also remembered that he had 'stood strong'. The Buddhist made air quotes here with a small smile, feeling a little political or like a boxing trainer. He then advised Elise Grantwell to do the same, to 'stand strong', again air quoting. Elise Grantwell nodded and opened her mouth to talk. For instance, the Buddhist continued, when my mother claimed that she had lost a son to a cult, I responded by saying to her, I'm sorry I can't satisfy what you want me to be, but I have no one to satisfy except myself and may you one day realize the same. The Buddhist said how he remembered very clearly using the word 'may'. May you one day realize the same, he said into his screen, playing with the fabric of his robes. It was a ridiculous and condescending way to put it, he said. I was a little attached to the whole Buddhist thing. It made me talk like an idiot. Elise Grantwell laughed in a way that a person laughs when they're trying to show just how comfortable and not insecure they are, the Buddhist observed. He noticed this while at the same time choosing to ignore it, then calmly recalled to Elise Grantwell how his mother had cried a little when he had said this, then how she had slapped him. Such a shock. His mother, he recalled, who was a small, waifish woman who would die of cancer while the Buddhist was teaching in Sri Lanka, had never struck the Buddhist before, even as a child. After striking the Buddhist, his mother's eyes had looked into the Buddhist's eyes, as if searching for the lost former self of her son, the Buddhist recalled. I stood looking at her, calm and accepting, while she cried, the Buddhist told Elise Grantwell. My cheek burning. In the kitchen of the family's house, my father's house. My father was standing in the corner of the kitchen, stroking his beard, a thing he always did in moments of either conflict or reflection. I remember how he gave me a stare of pure anger and hatred. Such a disgusting stare that I actually lost my composure. I got really angry at him and said, You look like an animal right now.

For a moment, the Buddhist thought he was going to throw up. He put his hand to his mouth; Elise Grantwell asked if he was okay; the feeling passed, and he told Elise Grantwell he had been throwing up all night. Oh my God, she said. You should lie down, you don't need to be talking to me. The Buddhist said he was fine. It was just an unpleasant feeling and would pass. The Buddhist said this, aware that he was using his physical ailment to teach a lesson of impermanence and non-attachment to thoughts, feelings and physical sensations to Elise Grantwell, as if his body and being were the textbook from which Elise Grantwell was studying. Suddenly, the Buddhist had a terrible desire to scratch his back, and at the same time felt a wave of fever run up his spine and into his head, which made his eyes water. The computer screen blurred in his vision. He closed his eyes hard and took a sip of water, hoping that it wouldn't make him want to vomit. When he opened his eyes, the room spun slightly, moving from left to right, left to right, and the Buddhist closed his eyes again. He waited a moment, following his breath. When he opened his eyes, Ajahn was looking into the hall. Feel okay? he said in English, a subtle yet generous gesture of compassion. The Buddhist nodded. Food soon, Ajahn said. Cook is waking up from drink. Outside, the day was warming and insects were wildly buzzing and the humidity of the forest seemed to be overtaking the cooling of the air conditioning.

This is all on my mind, said the Buddhist to Elise Grantwell, turning back to his screen, because I'm returning to my home country, to people who had a difficult time accepting me, so all these things that you're going through are also very appropriate for me, said the Buddhist. It's a wonderful lesson for both of us. Elise Grantwell's face distorted into pixelation – the connection seemed like it was about to be lost – but then resolved into clarity. The Buddhist continued by saying that he remembered, shortly after his mother slapped him, that his father had said, privately, away from his mother so as not to upset her more, that he didn't understand how his son, a remarkable person, always a wonderfully caring and selfless individual, could have become so selfish. He said, When did you turn into such a pretentious and condescending shit, not to mention a bum? Look at all this we've given you. We've given you everything, he had said, indicating the house and the material possessions of which his parents were, the Buddhist explained, overly proud.

It was about that time, the Buddhist said, that my father told me to get out of his house, which my father had designed and built and kept up and which I had, he told me, lost the right to live in. Which my mother of course protested. To which my father responded by saying things like, Fine, if you want to let him hurt you repeatedly and without end, fine, go ahead. I'm done. The Buddhist recalled to Elise Grantwell, whose mouth was now agape on his screen, how he had simply walked out of the kitchen to meditate in his bedroom and then packed to leave.

ALAN ROSSI

Elise Grantwell said, Wow. The Buddhist saw Elise Grantwell
adjust her camera so that it showed more of her upper body and
her breasts beneath a tight white oxford shirt. The Buddhist could
see her bra through the oxford and noted, with surprise, that her
breasts, for a forty-year-old woman, were still very full and pleasant
and attractive. The Buddhist observed his sexual feelings with calm
detachment, noting that because Elise Grantwell's camera was now
more focused on her face and body, which was attractive, that he felt
both an attraction toward her and an aversion toward the attraction.
He allowed the feelings to pass.

Oh, I forgot the best part, the Buddhist said. On his screen, Elise
Grantwell perked up, sitting more upright, which almost caused the
Buddhist to say that she looked better when she sat up straight. He
observed that in the box of the screen he remained composed and
uninterested in Elise Grantwell's appearance. The Buddhist realized
that he needed to acknowledge that part of the reason he enjoyed
talking to Elise Grantwell was the fact that she was, by conventional
social standards, a pretty woman and he liked the attention she gave
him. He noted this and tried to understand that his real position here
was situated in the universal, helping to usher Elise Grantwell to the
shore of non-suffering. The Buddhist allowed himself to focus on
his duty. He then recalled with sarcastic humor to Elise Grantwell
that the best part of the whole thing was that before he returned to
Sri Lanka to live the rest of his life as a monk, his parents had held a
family meeting with the former girlfriend the Buddhist had broken
up with to be a Buddhist. An intervention for a Buddhist, he said to
Elise Grantwell, who smiled and laughed overly sincerely. It instantly
passed through the Buddhist's mind, stopping him completely,
like pausing a YouTube video, that Elise Grantwell found the
Buddhist attractive – her eyes rarely holding his stare, her general
discomfort and insecurity coupled with her need to impress, her
frequent movement of body and straightening of her back – all of
it suddenly and intuitively seemed to the Buddhist to be her sexual
reaction to him, though she may not have acknowledged it

160

consciously. The Buddhist also understood, just as instantly, that even if this were true, all he could do was what he was already doing – it was not related to him, was not his concern, was causing Elise Grantwell suffering, and itself was fleeting and no-self.

The Skype connection went choppy. Elise Grantwell's face morphed into three pixelated blocks of color, green, blue and black, like a puzzle the Buddhist would have to put back together. Then a moment later the bad connection resolved and there was her face, alien and lost and concerned, staring at him from a different part of the Skype window. There was a counselor present at the family meeting, the Buddhist said. She was this weary and hardened woman of about sixty. With serious wrinkles and a set of dentures that protruded from her greatly sagging face, a former addict who usually intervened in substance abuse, the Buddhist explained. So, my family had hired this counselor woman because my parents and former girlfriend considered me *addicted* to a cult/religion. So, there I was, in my saffron robes, sitting on one side of the family's kitchen table, and then my parents were like really close together, very tense and concerned and clearly not getting any sleep, the Buddhist explained, smirking a little while he explained, and then there was my former girlfriend, who, I remember, was very confused, probably because I was not having sex with her and was wearing somewhat creepy robes and had actually broken up with her. Elise Grantwell responded by laughing exaggeratedly, which the Buddhist was annoyed by, but which he also knew was born out of her attempt to connect, to show the Buddhist she was paying attention. He met her exaggerated laughs with composure and equanimity and acceptance.

His mother, father and ex-girlfriend sat opposite him on the other side of the table, a very fine, very heavy oak table with marble inlaid flowers at the corners. The wearied gray-haired counselor woman had said: Sean, these people have something to say to you. And I remember the counselor was also looking a little confused, the Buddhist said. Because here I was, very healthy, very in control, and once they all began talking – saying I was lost, saying I was selfish, saying I was hurting all of them, saying I was addicted to a cult, asking what had happened to my passion for life, for playing music and kayaking, for enjoying expensive meals, saying how they had lost a son, had lost a boyfriend, had lost a friend – among all this I maintained an accepting and calm demeanor, and I think this wearied former-addict counselor started to get that maybe my parents, my mother especially, were the ones who actually needed help. Like they were the desperate ones. Anyway, this counselor eventually ended the intervention, the Buddhist said. She said that she was misled and she wasn't needed here, the Buddhist said while Elise Grantwell smiled and said, Oh, wow, wow. It was both a little victory and painful at the time, the Buddhist explained to Elise Grantwell, because I think it distanced me further from my family, or my family distanced themselves further from me. But the point is that I can look back at it with detachment and humor.

So what did you tell them? Elise Grantwell wanted to know. What was said at the intervention that made the counselor know you were right? The Buddhist thought for a moment, vaguely interested in Elise Grantwell's question. He then realized that she wanted an answer, something clear and definitive, that she might repeat to others. It wasn't a question of right and wrong, the Buddhist said. I'm just curious about what you said, Elise Grantwell told him in a very quiet, almost embarrassed way. Well, he said, he had tried to calmly explain to his parents, who were not yet divorced, to his mother who was not yet dead, to his father who was not yet only speaking to him through Post-it notes, that he had no beliefs in particular, he didn't believe in a god, he didn't have any particular kind of faith, that that wasn't what Buddhism was about. As the Buddhist explained this, he watched Elise Grantwell and felt that perhaps she was not sexually attracted to him but that, because of the materialistic and sexually objectifying culture she lived in, she was conditioned, in some basic and unconscious way, to present herself, in any situation, as a sexual object; she looked very pretty, he thought, while also thinking that he didn't like her insecurity, over-sincerity or the fact that she was trying to impress him by asking more and more questions and appearing more and more interested. Though of course, he instantly thought, maybe she genuinely wanted an answer, some simple answer to an equation that would solve her life. Additionally, he told Elise Grantwell, I tried to explain to them that this was about seeing into the reality of life, the nature of the mind and how to end suffering; that it was all very logical and required no mysticism or transcendence or belief in things that didn't exist. That's probably when the counselor decided to leave, the Buddhist said.

The Buddhist felt weak, nauseated, extremely sweaty and at the same time itchy. Again the need to vomit came and passed. The Buddhist used Mahasi Sayadaw's technique, inwardly labeling his sensations 'pain, itchiness, nausea'. There were of course protests, the Buddhist said. But you're like a machine now, his mother had said again and again. The Buddhist shrugged a little for Elise Grantwell to see. There's no joy of life in you, his mother had protested. My father told me that I was confused. He repeatedly told me that I was confused and on a fool's errand, that was the phrase he used, fool's errand, as if there could be a bigger fool's errand than continuing to live in a materialistic and oppressive society. A hard and stabbing ache made him close his eyes for a moment. Before he stopped talking to me, before I returned to Sri Lanka, my father liked to talk to me late at night and say very clichéd things, like, What about all the years at school? You have a promising career in front of you. You'd be a great psychiatrist or something like that. You know, I always wanted grandchildren. What about the family name? All those things, the Buddhist said, waving his hands at the world around him. Probably many things you're encountering as well, the Buddhist said to Elise Grantwell, who nodded and said, Oh yes, very much so, yes.

What about your partner? Elise Grantwell asked. The Buddhist withheld a sigh – he was tired, nearly exhausted, and the room had begun spinning again. The light from the computer screen was hard to look at. He dimmed the screen. From the kitchen, pots made clattering sounds and he smelled rice. He felt a terrible need to go to the bathroom and vomit, though such a thought was fearful. He also just didn't want to move at all. She called me the feeling police, the Buddhist said. Elise Grantwell laughed what the Buddhist felt was maybe the first actual laugh she had laughed all day, which he found pleasant, attractive, and he felt the need to make her laugh that way again. He told Elise Grantwell that after he was kicked out of his parents' house, before returning to Sri Lanka to stay at the temple for good, he stayed with his former girlfriend. It was a truly terrible idea, the Buddhist said. I actually found out later that my parents and girlfriend had like conspired; they had told her to get me to stay; they even gave her money, on the pretense that they were paying for my 'rent'. It did not go well, the Buddhist said. She tried to have conversations like we'd once had. She tried to flirt with me. I don't know, the Buddhist said, feeling depleted and nauseated. The Buddhist remembered how she wore sexually revealing clothes, exposing her legs and cleavage. She vacuumed in the nude once, the Buddhist said, which seemed pathetically desperate and sad. The Buddhist noticed that Elise Grantwell looked down more and kind of folded into herself, like the leaves of some plants in Sri Lanka that closed into themselves at night.

He said he told his girlfriend that she couldn't do things like that around monks. His girlfriend had said, I'm not around monks, I'm around you, *Sean*. What did you say to her? Elise Grantwell asked, quietly. The Buddhist shrugged. He had tried to explain to his girlfriend the new way he was following and he had decided to show her how this way could apply to her own life. Whenever she came home upset from work, whenever she was depressed about her life, whenever she was in a dark place, I tried to show her that her feelings contained no reality, they were impermanent, based on the belief of a false self. Elise Grantwell nodded vigorously while also adjusting herself on her cushion and rubbing one of her knees, as if one of her legs was asleep. Elise Grantwell listened and rubbed at the same time. The Buddhist said that he tried to show his former girlfriend, while he stayed in her apartment, that her feelings and thoughts, especially about the current situation between them, were clearly leading to her suffering and that she needed to see into the truth of reality, which was the first line from the Dhammapada, that what the mind is, the world is. She was creating her own suffering, to which his girlfriend had replied, No, Sean, *you're* creating my fucking suffering. The Buddhist recalled that they had sat on her sofa often while he tried to teach her these things, but she just couldn't understand.

What'd she do? Elise Grantwell wanted to know. She told me, often through tears, that she missed Sean, that I wasn't Sean anymore, I was trying to control her and make her a Buddhist or something, when her feelings were real, her thoughts were real, they were the only real things. Elise Grantwell looked down. The Buddhist said that he knew that he had to go back to Sri Lanka right away when his girlfriend interrupted his meditation by kissing his neck, which he tried to calmly move away from, and then reached her hand down his robe, grabbing hold of his penis and telling the Buddhist that this is what she missed too. The Buddhist laughed a slight, embarrassed laugh. Elise Grantwell kept her eyes down. Do you ever miss sex? she asked. The Buddhist, who observed that his face was neutral and calm, was surprised by the question. He said, I miss the idea, sometimes, or maybe the idea of being with another person, of, the Buddhist said, like, um, sharing with them or something. He was unsure of what he was saying. He stopped, composed himself, inwardly thinking 'confused, confused', and said, I don't miss the pleasure of sex because pleasure is fleeting, and therefore I understand it's nothing to miss, though, he admitted, perhaps I miss just closeness, maybe, though that could happen in different ways, the Buddhist said, a little exasperatedly. Elise Grantwell said that that made sense, qualifying the response with, for a monk.

The Buddhist thought for a minute, and then said he was sorry, he would be right back. He hurried to the bathroom, where he vomited.

Each retching seemed too fast to keep up with, more intensely uncontrollable than the last. He vomited and vomited again. After the third time it was watery and thin. He sat, half lying, on the floor of the bathroom, his hands shaking. He felt cooler, the only good part about it. On the floor, he checked his robes to make sure no vomit had gotten on them. He cleaned partially digested chunks of rice and vegetables off the toilet lid, flushed, and washed his hands and face, feeling shaky and weak and wanting never to vomit again, knowing that such a selfish want was based on ignorance.

The Buddhist returned to his spot before the laptop. Elise Grantwell was saying how sorry she was, she could let him go, and the Buddhist put a hand up, palm out, and said it was all right, such things happened, and they were almost finished anyway. What should she do? Elise Grantwell wanted to know. The Buddhist said the best thing to do was very little. Just keep practicing and living and doing, he said. The Buddhist said that the last time he saw his entire family and girlfriend, nearly five years ago now, before he had gone back to Sri Lanka for what he thought would be the remainder of his life, before his mother had died and his father had stopped speaking to him, he said that they had all had a brunch together. My father sat quietly in his seat, less stoic than confused, he told her. My girlfriend was pale and quiet. My mother was just reserved and sad-looking. I remember how I said that if they could see from my position that they were being pulled around by their emotions, their feelings and their thoughts, if they could see this truth in the same way I could, then they would understand why I was doing what I was doing, and also, more importantly, if they could see this, they wouldn't be suffering as they were right at that moment. I told them they were causing their own suffering, and I felt for all of them. None of them responded. Then my father drove me to the airport. It was a terribly lonely time, the Buddhist said.

It was dengue. The Buddhist had probably contracted it when he was meditating in the forest near the stream, where the mosquito population was dense and the insects were large and aggressive. A doctor came from the village and told the Buddhist and the other monks that the Buddhist could not, by any means, travel, and that what the Buddhist needed was to go to the hospital and get a saline drip right away because he was more than a little dehydrated. The doctor conveyed his irritation at the monks by speaking sternly, abruptly, and slamming things in and out of his bag. The Buddhist could hear and perceive very little when the doctor visited; his fever was dangerously high, causing strange hallucinations (he believed, for instance, that he was back in his father's house, which had somehow been turned into an eighteen-hole golf course, and he kept asking the monks what hole his mother was on), intense and bewildering nightmares concerning a tricycle-cum-lawn-mower, and now diarrhea along with the vomiting. Ajahn said they would begin their walk to the city tomorrow. Tomorrow?, the doctor said. Walk? Ajahn replied that the doctor must know that monks were not allowed to ingest any kind of medicine unless it was absolutely necessary, nor were they allowed any medical help unless it was absolutely called for, and were meant to experience the reality of suffering in order to be free of the fact of suffering. The doctor shoved his things into his case and then left, proclaiming that if the young Canadian Buddhist died Ajahn would live countless lives in Hell, to which Ajahn replied, That's it, my friend!

A rickshaw driver saw the monks as they walked to the hospital. He helped the monks cart the sick Buddhist. It was a day and a half's walk and they stopped and begged along the way and families came out, bowing to the monks and making offerings of rice and fish. The rickshaw man often bowed to the monks, who grew tired of bowing back. The Buddhist could not bow back; his thin body was thinner, paler, his eyes red and deeply sunken into his head, a white crust at the corners of his lips.

At the hospital, two nurses hurried him to a bed and began a saline drip. The Buddhist dreamed it was snowing. In the dream, the Buddhist sat next to his father while it snowed and his stepmother sat across from them. There was oatmeal with pieces of apple and brown sugar in a bowl before the Buddhist. The bowl was melting the snow. In the dream, the Buddhist was telling his father he was not supposed to eat any food given to him unless it was given with three bows, but the Buddhist's father was no longer sitting next to him. The Buddhist was momentarily walking inside a shopping mall, looking into each store, though he didn't know what for. Then the Buddhist was back in the deep, snowing woods. The Buddhist's father was suddenly there again, eating a bowl of oatmeal, but with his back facing the Buddhist. The Buddhist tried to get around his father to see his face, but as he moved around him he realized his father only had a back, had no face. The Buddhist's faceless father nodded, finished his oatmeal and took his plate to a sink in the middle of the snowing woods and washed the plate and then just stood there.

The doctor explained to the Buddhist that the Buddhist was probably feeling better. The doctor walked to the edge of the bed and felt the Buddhist's forehead with the back of his hand. He moved away again. The doctor said the Buddhist was feeling better because of the saline drip, but that such a feeling was misleading and the dengue would get worse before it got better. Not only that, the hospital was running low on saline; in fact, the doctor said matter-of-factly, they were out. More would arrive, but not until tomorrow afternoon. Dengue is biphasic, he said. You've just finished the first phase. The second phase will begin any moment now. The Buddhist said okay and explained that he felt better and he was grateful to the doctor. The doctor stood there as though he had something else to add. The Buddhist said, Say it. The doctor said it was not his place to say anything and then said that it was foolish, all of it, and after looking at the Buddhist for a moment, closed the curtain and went out.

He opened his laptop again and saw that Elise Grantwell was contacting him through Skype. Her face resolved on his screen, asking how he was. He told her he felt tired, but was fine. At the same moment, he saw his father was trying to connect with him, but he ignored the call and focused on Elise Grantwell, who was thanking the Buddhist for all his help, telling him he had helped her to understand that there is a difference between being lonely and being alone, and that one is always and forever alone, but loneliness is the extra, the part that's unnecessary, and she saw that now. She continued talking, but he didn't hear her, was instead watching his father's Skype icon blinking on the screen next to Elise Grantwell's face. The Buddhist felt what seemed like a fist lodged near his heart. Then Elise Grantwell was saying, What's wrong? What is it? The Buddhist shook his head. Why are you crying? she said. What is it? ∎

The Emotional Life of Plants

An exciton consists
of the escaped negative
(electron)
and the positive hole
it left behind.

This binary system
is unstable
and must be transported quickly
to the processing center
which, in practice, means
the exciton must be left
strictly alone
so that it travels
all ways at once
going nowhere
but also
going directly
to the factory floor.

Leaving aside the question
of what it means
for a positive hole
to be 'left behind'
and also to travel
as half of a system,
this happens because nothing
can be still
and because, for the lonely,
direction is meaningless.

OLD-AGE RAGE

Daisy Jacobs

All winter, I've been sleeping in the room I slept in as a child and I wake up each day not knowing how old I am. Five? Or twenty-five? He could live to be a hundred – I could be middle-aged, still staring up at this same ceiling.

'Go in and see your grandad,' Mum says as I come downstairs. 'The carers are late.'

'He's shat himself,' she adds, in passing.

I make myself go in, make myself touch and hold the shaking hand on the duvet, weightless as a husk. Our hands shake in unison.

'Try not to move too much,' I shout as the flat screen roars and holds his attention like a jealous God. *Rogue Traders, Flog It!* PPI. 'Send us your unwanted gold.'

I hate it in here. I foam with hatred at the grip bars, the Tena pants, the strew of hard crumbling tissues, corn plasters on saucers, hearing aids gouted in soft brown wax, missed pills, food stains, giant multi-packs of laxatives; I hate the stairlift, the ramps, the beep-beep-beep of his wheelchair, and the all-pervading smell of shit. I hate his scabs, his dribble, his pee, right here in the bedside bottle, dark and pungent as chip-shop vinegar. This is not my grandad.

'He's not himself,' Mum says in the kitchen. Well, who is he then? Is he 40 per cent of his young self? Ten? Do I still have to love him as much as ever, this 90 per cent stranger?

One afternoon, I take him out for a walk in his chair.

'I strained,' he yells, 'and strained – '

The cold comes in off the flat grey water as we toil along the deserted promenade, and a clean wind scatters the endless saga of his bowels.

'Go in and sit with him while I make lunch, will you, love?'

I take in the daily paper he can't even read – *Macular degeneration. Wet. Incurable, I'm afraid* – and watch him shuffle the broadsheets of pulsing copy as his sight leaks away through the back of his eyeballs. Even the house is dying – old furniture slipping away, room by room. The big bed, the little velvet love seat – gone now, making way for cankers of dead-salmon-pink plastic and power-coated steel. We have furniture with motors, apparatus for making all the moves I selfishly take for granted: a carousel for turning, a hoist and sling for lifting the body and separating it from its waste or settling it in bed, after ten hours in a chair. And all the time the televisions multiply and grow. He never seems to tire of it, unless we're busy; then he switches it off and sits in wait, contact-hungry and silently annoying. Where has everyone gone? Why is Mum alone with the soiled sheets, the six tiny meals a day, painstakingly prepared and refused with a petulant 'No' – alone with the fetching, the shopping, the washing, the phoning, the doctor's calls, the endless 'cup of tea?'s and the smell? And the suspicion in the watery bird's eyes that it is all for our benefit. Or is it fear? Fear of being left to die like a sick beast? I want to die like an animal. I will walk into the woods, swim out to sea. But what if I, too, am paralysed, my spine crumbling like a packet of biscuits, or dementia gets me, my own aspirin-thinned blood rinsing myself from the crevices of my brain – what then?

The rustling has stopped; he's peering fiercely from the ruins of the paper.

'Is that you, Eiley? Are you there?'

I hope not; she's been dead three years.

'It's just me,' I say, suppressing the urge to look behind me.

'There was a time she came out of . . . where she put . . . you remind me . . . you've got the same colouring . . . she just put her hand up and waved . . .'

He stares at me for a long time, smiling. I wish he'd hurry up and die.

And suddenly he says it – my name, says it as though I've just come into the room, not been stuck here for months, says it as though *he*'s been here all the time. I can see in his eyes that it's him looking out at me, really him. And then he's gone again.

'I can't leave him,' Mum says. And, 'I don't know what I'd do without you.'

I make us all a drink. As the kettle boils, I wonder: what do we mean by love?

Three coffees, black, no sugar. I take them through, and our life sentences run on, concurrently. ■

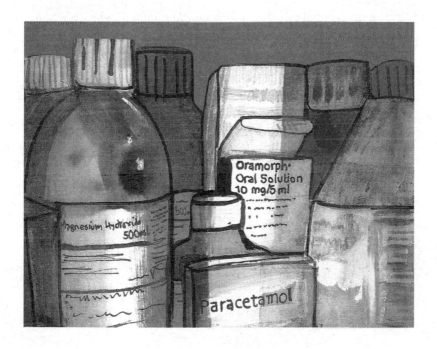

© PAOLO ČERIĆ

POSSESSION

Bella Pollen

The demon came as demons do, during the faithless hours of early morning. I'd been ascending through ever shallowing layers of sleep when finally I breached the surface. I stretched for my phone and groaned. 4 a.m. is a brutal time to wake up. Too late for a sleeping pill, too early for a new day. I shut my eyes again but almost at once the usual worries began crowding me, quickly magnifying from the banal to the absurd. *What if the accumulation of everything I've learned adds up to nothing? What if the story I've sold myself about life isn't the real story? What if I'm dying of that rare kidney disorder I read about in Time last week?* 4.02. A branch tapped against the curtainless window. Outside was wintry black. The night had a child's-picture-book quality to it: a waxing gibbous moon, spores of mist drifting through it. The air became eerily still and for a moment I felt dislocated, suspended in time. My insomnia makes me vulnerable to the tricks night plays, so I wiggled my toes under the blankets; then, reassured I was awake, resolved to count my way back to sleep on the rhythm of tiny taps and creaks generated by the silence. I was close to succeeding too when I heard something, at first faintly, then increasingly clearly – the tread of footsteps coming up the stairs.

My eyes snapped back open. I was alone on the property and this was the first night I'd slept there. The grounds were still a building site, my bed the only piece of furniture in the house. *This isn't right,* I told myself. I'd distinctly remembered locking doors and bolting windows. But – and this perhaps was the first sign that my thoughts were originating from a place below the level of conscious reasoning – instead of fear, I felt mild outrage, as though whatever was coming up those stairs was not playing fair, not playing by the rules. Somewhere deep inside me, I think I already knew that whatever I was dealing with was not human.

My husband and I had bought the property two years earlier and immediately begun renovations. To say that the project was stressful was a gross understatement. It was as though the house had been storing up its grievances for centuries, and now with every brick pulled was releasing them back upon us. Bats, rats, floods, rot – one by one they came, the seven plagues of Oxfordshire. The house was an old rectory next to a Norman church and graveyard. There was a sense of unrest about the graveyard's higgledy-piggledy layout, as if bodies and bones had been shifted to make room for newcomers and now the original occupants were muttering like angry commuters on a packed train. It was possible, I suppose, that this honey-coloured village had been an idyll for milkmaids marrying their farming loves, but it was equally likely that it had been a finger-pointing, witch-burning community, meting out who knew what kind of innovative torture in the name of God. Long before the footsteps started up the stairs, I'd wondered whether the place might be haunted.

I became aware of a presence in the room. The side of my bed dipped as if someone had sat down heavily. Arms encircled me from behind. I felt the embrace of pins and needles as a body pressed against mine. It seemed to be made of iron filings – millions of them, detached, free moving, yet somehow magnetically drawn together into a human shape. I never saw it, but this was the image that developed in my head as the arms gathered me in. Good God, was it spooning me? For the first time in a long time I felt cherished and safe. Tears blurred my eyes. I was exhausted, demoralised, struggling to finish a novel. The building project had caused so much antipathy between my husband and me that we were barely speaking, let alone spooning. I sighed. The arms tightened in response, as if aware of the comfort they were giving. I sighed again. Again the arms tightened – the iron filings moving fluidly into the gap left by my exhalation. I pushed out against my diaphragm but once again, as my lungs deflated, the space was stolen from me. I began to panic. Whatever this thing was, it was not benign. I called out but no sound came. I tried to break free but found I could move neither my arms nor my legs. Soon I could no longer breathe. Pressure rose in my chest. I'd experienced something similar to this once before – after the delivery of my first child by Caesarean. Something went wrong while they were stitching me up and the pressure had built, culminating in a tremendous burst of pain in my heart. Simultaneously I heard the beep of the monitor flatlining. As medics pounced, some misplaced survival instinct told me they were trying to kill me and I'd fought them with the last of my strength. Now I did the same – mustering something internal, something almost telekinetic. There was a rushing in my ears, I felt the violent throwback of an explosion and, suddenly, I was free.

In the bathroom, I splashed cold water onto my face and stared into the mirror. My skin was the colour of parchment, my eyes flat.

I've always suffered from nightmares. I can't tell you the multitude of ways I've watched my family being dispatched to their graves over the years. I've seen my brother hanging bloodied out of the mouths of monsters, a faceless woman leading my mother away, my son waving at me, then turning to jump to his death down a bottomless black hole. Nor am I merely a spectator at the horror show of my subconscious: my hands have been chewed off by creatures of the deep, my eyes prised from their sockets by gelatinous fingers. In one of my cheerier recurring dreams I am forced to walk down a narrow corridor whose walls are a pulsing, rippling lattice of serpents, some oily and brown, others speckled and wickedly fluorescent, all with tongues that flick out as I pass. Like the video game whose next level is unattainable, I am invariably struck before I reach safety.

I have tried to understand the psychology of these nightmares and the experiences that fuel them. Humans, of course, are born with an evolutionary bias that predisposes us to fear any creature that poses a threat. Estimates put snakebites at around 5.5 million a year, resulting in 125,000 deaths, 30,000 of which are in sub-Saharan Africa alone. That's a lot of venom, but then I don't live in sub-Saharan Africa; I live in London. What I had was a rational fear repeated in an irrational setting – in other words, a phobia.

There's a school of psychoanalysis that suggests that something grisly in childhood accounts for adult obsession and fears. My mother grew up in Africa, and certainly her stories of being chased across the plains by the black mamba were the stuff of bedtime legend. Closer to home, I remember running barefoot through the long grass at my grandmother's house and seeing the writhing coils of mating grass snakes below me. In that one airborne second, I managed to adjust my trajectory. Grass snakes are harmless, amiable creatures; nevertheless I later felt sick at how close I'd come to landing on that foul, spongy mass. Further back still there had been a strange incident at the Bronx Zoo. A cobra, demented by captivity, had repeatedly bashed itself against the glass of its cage. Even as my mother tried to pull me away, I'd stood my ground, as fascinated as I was scared. So, yes, snake nightmares I could account for – as for the rest, who knew? Not that it was relevant anyway, because the iron filings had been no nightmare. It had happened while I was awake.

'Fuck,' I said to my reflection. 'Fuck fuck fuck.'

4.20 a.m. No possibility of sleep now. Back in bed, I tried to regulate my breathing but after a while became aware of my body feeling fractionally out of sync with its surroundings. A branch scraped against the window – the Maurice Sendak world of moons and interwoven fairy tales knocking to come in. Again the air went still. *No*, I thought, *please no!* I wiggled my toes under the covers and looked round the room. Everything was as it should be: the edge of the fireplace, the splintery uncarpeted floorboards, my hand raised in the gloamy light.

This time when the bed dipped, I felt a burning sensation on my skin. Arms closed around me and tightened. Overwhelmed by a sense of inevitability, I felt myself soften. The pressure began building, quicker this time, more urgently, but instead of fear or panic I felt a savage, primordial arousal, then the sensation of being penetrated, utterly possessed, before the unstoppable rush to orgasm, as intense as it was short, after which, once again, spell broken, I found myself alone.

Everyone relishes a good haunting story. *Bella has a sex ghost.* The delighted whisper came back to me full circle within the week. Suggestions poured in. I should hire a paranormal investigator, approach the local priest. Friends recommended their exorcist in the same casual manner they might have passed on their plumber or family doctor. By the time my dentist, who'd just completed a course in hypnotherapy, offered to have strict words with my subconscious, I was so unsettled by all the teasing that when he told me to relax and find a happy place, the best I could come up with was the chocolate-croissant counter in Pret A Manger. During all this, there were two more visits, both at 4 a.m., both while I was awake. On each occasion, the *presence* – as it was now officially known – returned a few minutes after I had initially broken free to push into the empty crevices of my body, take me to the edge of the sexual abyss and then carelessly drop me over, adding a frisson of shame to what was already a profoundly frightening experience. I was raped, brutalised. The creature had worked its full will upon my body and yet, yet . . . I'd taken pleasure in it?

It was left to my friend, a journalist and polymath, to identify the problem. 'What you've described,' he said over dinner, 'is a classic visitation from an incubus.'

I Wikipediaed 'incubus'. Under a helpfully graphic image of a satanic creature hovering over a prone unconscious female were the words: 'An incubus is a demon in male form who lies upon sleepers, especially women, in order to engage in sexual activity with them.' Attributed to everything from incest to the slovenly habit of eating in bed, the appearance of the incubus turns out to be a phenomenon in every corner of the globe. The Ecuadorian Tintín, for instance, is said to be a dwarf with a penchant for overly hairy women whom he serenades with a guitar. In Brazil, the Boto is a dolphin in the form of a beautiful man who, when dragging his women to the river, considerately wears a hat to disguise his blowhole. Germanic folklore tells of a winged goblin that rides on the chest of humans while they sleep. And so it goes on, round the world – imps, jinns and spirits from South Africa to Russia. Cultural and mythological variations aside, all incubi come with the same dread warning on the label: 'Repeated sexual activity with them may result in the deterioration of health, or even death.'

Thoroughly spooked, I moved the bed into a different room and refused to sleep alone in the house. After the building project was completed, I went to Australia to finish my book. A new country, new people, new sounds and smells – Australia was escape and escape is my oxygen. I hadn't thought about the incubus for months, when somewhere north of Adelaide, alone in a sweet roadside motel, I woke to a sense of heightened unreality and the presence between my thighs. I reached down in protest and the unmistakable iron fingers closed over my hand and pushed me away.

By the end of that year, having experienced three more visitations in Mexico, in Colorado, in Afghanistan – all places I had gone to lose myself – I understood with a terrible clarity that I couldn't outrun this thing. Wherever I went, however far I travelled, there it was, next to me on the aeroplane, unfolding its iron-filing legs, reading the in-flight magazine and ordering the chicken or fish. There was no demon living in the spare room of a Cotswold house back in England. The demon lived inside me.

In the panoply of the supernatural, possession is one of the more terrifying concepts: the idea of something lurking inside you, something inherently evil, something that can't be controlled or killed off. I thought about my other phobias and the stories that I had collected around them. The Chinese man with a live worm eating through his brain; the woman who had swallowed a snake egg in a river in India that hatched inside her, coiling around her organs, stealing into the hollow spaces of her body until, eventually, on the white sheets of the operating table, unable to move or breathe, she'd died – no longer human but merely the shell, the husk of a malevolent guest.

Poltergeist, Paranormal Activity, The Devil Inside. Like everyone else, I'd watched these horror flicks through spread fingers, laughing nervously at the pastiche of the woman in her white nightie – haunted, controlled, before finally being dragged across the bedroom, her nails leaving raw scratch marks on the wooden boards. Suddenly it all felt very close to home. Paranoia is not good for insomnia. I shut windows, slept with the lights on, tuned the audio of my hearing to its most sensitive frequency to listen for signs of unlawful entry. Nothing helped. It wasn't long before I found myself caving in to the self-pitying mantra of the victim: *why me?*

The upside of being a writer is that whatever answers you're unable to find within your own life, you can simply make up. I decided to stop feeling sorry for myself. If the thing was feeding on fear, I would make light of it; better still, mock it. I'd exorcise my incubus by writing the thing clean out of me. I began working on a comic novel about a depressed obsessive–compulsive who falls in love with his succubus, as the female of the species is known. She was fleshy, voluptuous and a marvellous cook, if something of a slob, who left crumbs in his bed and liked to eat Viennese Sachertorte in his bath.

I couldn't make a single story thread connect. Would my hero choose death and happiness with a figment of his imagination or the misery of life with his unloving, bloodless wife? Writers create characters and the world for them to inhabit, and usually it's a world so much more captivating than our own that we happily fall into it for years at a time. In this imaginary kingdom, we are the legislators of laws, the architects of every edifice. Writing fiction is the ultimate expression of megalomania, but when you've lost control of your own life, you lose the ability to puppeteer the lives of others.

The creative block that followed was both absolute and shattering.

Day after day I sat blankly at my desk while, like grain filling a barn, the iron filings continued to pour into the empty store of my imagination.

Repeated visits from an incubus can cause illness and sometimes death. Death of what? I thought bitterly.

My publishers were patient. My husband was practical. 'It'll come when it comes,' he said. I couldn't quite make him understand the problem. It wasn't just that I'd lost a muse; my muse had been replaced by a ravenous parasite.

And then I discovered science. How on earth did it take me so long to get there? In my defence I can only say that the mythological explanation of my demon was so uncannily accurate that it never occurred to me to look for another. But suddenly there it was on my screen, the result of a few minutes' distracted googling. 'Sleep paralysis is a state between wakefulness and sleep characterised by complete muscle atonia and often accompanied by terrifying hallucinations – specifically of an intruder in the room.'

Sleep paralysis always happens during REM – dream sleep – to prevent Tarantino-style carnage as we act out our nightmares. During REM, body and mind cooperate beautifully, ensuring that when the cycle finishes, so too does the paralysis. At least this is how it works for most people. For others – narcoleptics, night workers or unlucky souls such as myself – something goes awry. In our case, mind and body are not on speaking terms, allowing us to drift into sentience before the REM cycle has finished.

And it's at this point that the science gets really interesting. When we wake up paralysed we feel under threat, which, under normal circumstances, triggers a fight-or-flight reflex. Being paralysed, of course, we can do neither and this throws us into a state of terror. It turns out, however, that the brain is a bureaucratic organ with an almost neurotic determination to balance its books. To account to the department of logic for this terror, it calls on the office of imagination to conjure up a worthy vision. Enter the incubus, the malevolent intruder, the giggling goblin squatting on your chest. Enter your deepest terror, courtesy of your own subconscious.

So forget the monsters, the pulsing tapestry of snakes, forget the bottomless black hole. Though these too grew out of subconscious fears, they were subconscious fears in concert with recognisable outside influences, and they didn't leave any lasting impact on my psyche and soul. The incubus felt different. The incubus made me feel that the thing I was most frightened of was myself.

'You don't need an exorcist,' my husband told me. 'You need a good shrink.'

On the continuum of sanity I've always considered myself closer to normal than the twitchy loon of the asylum, plucking flies out of the air and eating them. Perhaps that sounds smug – or lacking in self-awareness – but on the whole I've always been pretty sure of who I am and what I believe. I hate bigots, snobs and ignorance, and even if the inside of my head is a pinboard of politically incorrect gags, snap judgements and coloured flash cards of what to eat for my next meal, that's a paradox I've learned to live with. Believe me, nothing any doctor can say is going to straighten out the kinks in those telephone wires.

I understand that psychoanalysis works miracles for some people, but I was brought up to believe that talking about yourself was the height of boorishness, not to mention very un-English. The suggestion that I should go out and find a shrink raised in me a whole new raft of anxieties. I have to admit that in general I'm leery of doctors and their credentials. You only have to look at my incubus to see I haven't always been the best picker of men. If the shrink I chose was subpar, he'd probably fall for my tricks and lies; if he was savvy enough to tap into the dark oily streams of my unconscious, chances are I'd be spending the rest of my days among the whispery chatter and muted shrieks of the Hospice de la Salpêtrière. I'm not sure I believe in the process of therapy either. However crooked the journey that brings us here, here is where we are, and to trawl through the past looking for someone to take the rap for the way you turned out seems neither fair nor right. I come from generations of pragmatic, stubborn DIY copers and I was determined to work this thing out myself.

Sleep paralysis was a stunning revelation. The scientific narrative stopped me from feeling like a crazy person. Once I stumbled over it, sleep paralysis was everywhere. In forums, medical journals, splashed over blogs. It even had its own documentary film about to premiere at Sundance. And take it back as far as you like: how many ghosts, how many Gothic stories and devils in literature could be attributed to it?

I decided to revisit some of the ghost stories that scared me as a teenager: *The Turn of the Screw*, *A Christmas Carol*, Edith Wharton's 'The Eyes'. It seemed to me that the last two were both cut-and-dried cases of sleep paralysis. Scrooge is haunted by his own greed and misanthropy, while Culwin's egotism is tormented by a pair of red eyes at the foot of his bed, which turn out to be the manifestation of his guilt and shame. It occurred to me that my 'ghost' might also be a metaphor for some secret if unexpressed emotion. Who hasn't at one point or another been possessed by the demons of jealousy, hatred, lust, low self-worth?

I don't consider myself an addict. I smoke a little, chug down the odd shot of alcohol and will happily swallow any pill that's slipped to me, but I can easily live without these things. Escape, running away, solitude: these are the highs I crave. When I'm at home I love everything it represents, but sooner or later it becomes too comfortable, too easy, and a fear of complacency sets in. I veer quickly from feeling safe and loved to feeling edgy, unable to breathe and finally so claustrophobic that I will do anything to break free – to experience the adrenaline and bliss of freedom.

And how compellingly similar was this pattern to the one of my haunting? I thought back to that day in the Bronx Zoo, standing hypnotised as the cobra banged its head against the glass in its determination to escape. The following day it had. The glass smashed, and the snake was gone. As a little girl this had terrified me. The serpent had had me in its sights, with every intention of hunting me down. But now I thought of it slithering through the unfamiliar streets of the city, excitedly taking in the new sights and smells, revelling in its liberty and independence. I fear that snake, but I understand it too. How long before it tired of freedom, before it curled up in an alley, cold and lonely, dreaming of a dead mouse and a dry cage? How long before it yearned to go home, back to the only place where things made sense?

This opposing pull between home and away has been the central struggle of my life for as long as I can remember. Addiction doesn't always come out of a bottle. It can be any habit that most adversely affects our behaviour, our sanity or the people around us. I have studiously avoided dealing with this issue, preferring instead to live in the eye of the storm, seeking out adventure and needless danger, immersing myself in worlds that are not my own and shutting myself off from the ones that are. I have driven my family crazy with this selfish behaviour until finally my guilt and unease began manifesting themselves in some sort of inhuman form. No wonder I couldn't move on. *Deal with me*, my demon is saying. *I am your demon and you need to pay attention to me or I will paralyse you forever.*

As a diagnosis, it's muddled, simplistic and moulded to the shape that suits me. Have I really dealt with the sexual aspect of it? Not even vaguely, but what does it matter? This is my demon. I conjured him up out of the nocturnal landscape of my own subconscious. The only person he has to answer to is me.

We still see each other from time to time, my incubus and I, though it's fair to say that some of the heat has gone out of our relationship. Sometimes I wake to find his hand on my shoulder before he slips away between the shadowy gaps of my sleep. Recently he's even acquired a sense of humour – should you choose to call it that. Earlier this year, as I felt his iron filings drain from my body, he touched the palm of my hand with his finger and said, 'You do know I'm married, don't you?' The day I began writing this piece, he appeared to me, no longer a collection of iron filings but made of flesh-coloured sandstone and, instead of a finger, he had a rotating drill on the end of his hand, which he extended towards me. 'Don't even think about it,' I said scornfully, and went back to sleep. Only later did the significance of this encounter occur to me: It was the first time I'd seen him, not as an image in my head, but as a 'real' entity outside it. Though in terms of recovery, arguably we still have some way to go, I took this as progress.

The truth is, I no longer wish to be rid of my demon. His visits always come when I'm alone, usually far from home, and they serve as a reminder to pay attention, not to mess with the balance of my life – and that makes him a friend, not an enemy. Besides, what's hidden deep inside us can also be the thing that drives us forwards. I've started working on a new project. A collection of non-fiction stories about a fickle, restless writer, forever probing new people and places. Even if the journey that has brought us here is crooked and can't be changed, I've decided it can't hurt to take a look at it. Books after all, are not unlike nightmares. They too can grow out of grisly past experiences. ∎

OPEN WATER

Deb Olin Unferth

By the next time she saw him she had discovered, without much
effort and without his knowing, his last name, then his entire
work history, previous places of residence, former wife's occupation
and location, children's names. She had seen photos of friends of
them all. She had learned about his penchants, his dreams, that he
believed in a benevolent God, that he enjoyed the open water of a
calm lake and the challenge of a narrow rapids. These facts in hand,
she had projected into the future what she might say to impress
him. She imagined being at his lonely bachelor pad in his four-story
apartment complex (she had studied pictures of the fountains and
two pools at the complex, of the weight room and the bike storage,
knew his probable rent, depending on whether he had two or three
bedrooms – or had he opted for only one?). She imagined his voice
getting gruffer as he told her his story (she knew he'd met his wife in
college and had married young, just two years after they'd finished
their degrees. Maybe they'd grown apart, maybe she'd left him, felt
she'd given him and their children her best years, willingly, but now
wanted more, and why not?). She imagined him telling her all this in
his kitchen, the new appliances, the island with its bar stools, going
over the facts she already knew. She saw his eyes on her slim body,
imagined him pulling her close (he had attended the university where

she now taught, and one of his sons was headed there now, the son who looked so much like him, same blue eyes, same thin neck, same tousled hair, a boy who'd won the eco-science fair that year, beat out fifty four other projects according to the Web announcement, was going places, this boy). She had already imagined it all, so much so that when she finally did see him, she felt unable to speak. Two short years back he'd had an awakening sweep over him, or a disaster befall him – she couldn't figure out which from the evidence. He'd left his place of employment after twelve years with the company, where he'd been such a presence, had been featured among the top executives in the country. But something had gone wrong: he'd divorced, made a move and it didn't seem lateral, though maybe it was, she really had no idea what any of it meant, the ridiculous job titles and descriptions that all sounded the same, vague and grandiose but also somewhat small in their ambitions.

He'd been through so much. They'd been through it, in a way, together, and now what was left? She felt far too intimate. They were long past pleasantries. If there was anywhere to go from here, it would be in silent understanding, the two of them on the shore of the lake where he weekly boated, or alone in one of his quiet rooms. But did she love him? Was he enough? Was she ready to disrupt the course of her life, become a stepmother to two teenagers, for this man, a man who loved water, who'd had children too young and now found himself at one end of a long corridor, more alone than he thought he'd be but ready for better: this man, cheerful, smiling nonchalantly? She wondered this when he arrived and she watched him across the room, talking to some of the others.

Alas, she already had the sick feeling of an ending inside her, the long sorrow of a slow break-up, of the impatience with which she would await his emails if he didn't write, her boredom with his boys (who played basketball and waterskied), their dislike of her and her efforts to assuage it – for what? For this blue-eyed man? She was so disappointed, in this, in them, had wanted much, was offering all, though he had asked for so little. Still she was willing to try. ∎

© ROMINA KHANOM
Women of Colour, 2014

THE MOTHER OF ALL SINS

Hanan al-Shaykh

TRANSLATED FROM THE ARABIC BY WIAM EL-TAMAMI

I lay in bed that first night at boarding school, listening to the silence wrap around me. Instead of hearing my father's voice chanting the *shahada* – 'There is no God but Allah, and Muhammad is His prophet' – I heard my own voice whispering: 'Mahdi, Mahdi, Mahdi – this is all because of you!'

My father's face turns bird-liver red. He attacks, raising his slipper high, a stray vein in his forehead throbbing. But the cockroach has already vanished, as though the earth had cracked open and swallowed it whole.

Shaking his head, my father murmurs the words he resorts to in moments of disappointment – 'There is no power but in God the Great' – before realising, in a panic, that he is still holding the slipper. He flings it to the floor and raises his hands to the ceiling – 'Forgive me, O Lord!' – then scrambles down on all fours, muttering the name of God the way we do when we've misplaced something, like the only comb in the house or the keys to the front door.

When he finally slumps out of the kitchen, dejected, it dawns on me that God has concealed the cockroach from my father because He has not forgiven him for uttering His name while holding a slipper. I lie down, pressing my cheek against the cold stone floor, murmuring the name of God with all my might so that He may guide me to the creature's hiding place.

Though I feel the revulsion human beings usually experience towards his species – especially since he was the type that had wings and could land, at any moment, on your head – I also feel a pang of sympathy. I recall all the times I had seen these creatures squashed, burned, drowned. The neighbour's son liked to deposit them in the ice compartment of the fridge and watch them slowly freeze to death.

And didn't God Himself create that cockroach, I suddenly think, just as He had created me? I was lucky: imagine being destined to a life of scurrying anxiously around and taking refuge in the most disgusting places, from the toilet bowl to the crack beneath the sink.

I peer under the cabinet and feel a rush of elation when I finally spot a pair of trembling whiskers. God has answered my prayer! Determined to save the cockroach and prove to Him that I could respect all His creatures, I heave myself up and reach for the *jinntass*.

For as long as I can remember, that magical copper bowl has been sitting in the same spot on the top shelf of the cabinet. On the outside it is etched with palm trees and mosques, inside with the outline of a hand filled with words that were a mystery to me until I was old enough to understand they were Quranic verses.

My mother believed that the words of God could bring calm to a frightened heart. She would fill up the bowl with water and bring it to me when I woke with a start in the night. She hurried to fill the bowl the day our neighbour, Suad, scrambled down from her balcony to ours to escape a burglar she'd found in her house.

My mother brought the bowl to her lips and the water splashed everywhere as Suad pushed it away, wailing: 'My leg! I've broken my leg! I beg you, take me to the doctor!'

I fill the bowl and place it at the foot of the cabinet, squeezing my eyes shut and hoping that the cockroach will drink the holy water.

The name of God had always echoed through our house: from the radio, from the minaret of the local mosque and from my parents' lips at every opportunity – my father when he caught a whiff of basil or mint, my mother when she saw her bread dough rising. They prayed to Him in feverish gratitude for giving them the gift of prayer.

But don't think I loved God any less than my parents, oh no. God was always with me. I saw His name sketched in the clouds that drifted across the sky; in the light pooling from the street lamp in our alley; in the pores of an orange, like eyes. Whenever I felt pain, I would put my hand on the spot where it hurt and repeat three times, 'In the name of God, Most Generous, Most Merciful.' And because God is God, and therefore male, I would apologise to Him, shamefaced, whenever I let out a fart or saw a few drops of pee on my underwear. And you shouldn't think that I was ignoring Him all those hours I spent doing my homework or daydreaming about boys or staring at my face in the mirror, wondering how to get rid of those tiny blackheads on my nose.

The cockroach didn't drink the water that day, and the following night I found his remains under my father's slipper. Before I could stop myself I went to my father, swept my arms wide and declared: 'Look, Father! Look at the spilled blood of that pitiful creature, the oozing guts! Did the Prophet himself not counsel us to lead animals gently to their death?'

I was trying to imitate Ustaz Najib, my Religious Studies teacher: the deep, rich tones of his voice and his enchanting language – an elaborate classical Arabic that was always laced with poetic images and studded with parables.

'My girls,' he would say, 'you must be as precious and rare as pearls, whether deep in the sea or safeguarded behind locked doors.'

But then, almost overnight, I was no longer the pearl in the Religious Studies lesson or the obedient girl at home. I had just turned fourteen and, although I still performed my daily prayers and wore skirts that reached down to my heels, I began to ignore my father when he told me to cover my mouth when I yawned so that the

Devil couldn't sneak in. I mocked my mother one day when she said that the minaret of the Ali ibn Abi Talib mosque sways or stands still depending on whether or not the oath taken before it was true.

My parents began to furrow their brows when they heard me giggling or humming a tune, wolfing down a piece of cake or admiring a dress in a shop window. My father would mutter that someone or something was leading me astray, and my mother would warn: 'Loving life is the mother of all sins.' I would think to myself: *But didn't God create jokes and cake and flower patterns too?*

And when my father told me to chant the *shahada* before I went to bed in case I died in my sleep, I didn't tell him what I was thinking. I didn't say that my nightie keeps away death, just like it kept away bedbugs. My aunt had brought it for me from Mecca, so the fabric was made of Quranic verses rather than threads. She was carrying it with her as she circled the Kaaba and threw stones at Satan. My parents had taken it with them when they went to the shrine of Sayyeda Zainab in Damascus, and they had wiped the tombs of the saints with it in Iraq.

And then the day came when I even refused to wear this beloved nightie of mine.

Ustaz Najib was teaching us the history of the imams.

'The twelfth imam, Muhammad ibn al-Hassan, was six years old when his father, the eleventh imam, Hassan al-Askari, passed away. Muhammad's uncle, Jaafar, was known as a devout man, a forsaker of earthly pleasures. He claimed the title of imam after his brother's death. But when Jaafar stood up to lead the funeral prayer, the child appeared and declared: 'Stand back, Uncle. I am more entitled than you to lead the prayer over my father's soul.' He led the town in prayer as confidently as an adult, to the astonishment of all, including his mother, Narjiss. After that, he disappeared under mysterious circumstances, an absence dictated by God, and in the end he will return, by the will of God, to establish a nation of righteousness and fill the world with justice and truth after it has become saturated with tyranny and debauchery.'

A classmate raises her hand and says: 'My father says that the imam was born in Samarra and went into a cave there and never came out.'

'There are many stories and predictions about Imam Muhammad ibn Hassan al-Askari, also known as the awaited Mahdi. The truth resides with God alone. Only He knows where His creatures are, even if one hides between a peanut and its shell.'

I suppress a laugh, remembering a neighbour of ours who would reply, when asked about her husband who had migrated to Africa: 'I'm waiting for the Mahdi to return.'

Then another thought occurs to me. I raise my hand.

'Sir, was the imam really six years old?'

'Yes, he was indeed . . . perhaps a year older or younger. What we can be sure of is that he disappeared at a very young age.'

I raise my hand again and have barely been given permission to speak when I blurt out: 'What about his mother? She must have been so worried!'

An image of Narjiss in her white mud hut began to form in my mind: searching frantically for her son, running towards the door – I could not imagine any windows – whenever she heard a sound. 'Mahdi! Mahdi!' she would call out, climbing a tree so that the wind would carry her call to him, wherever he was. And when the wind carried back nothing but the echo of her own voice, she would remember the neighbour who lost her son in the fish market and ran around looking for him, prising open the mouth of every big fish before finally going home to sit on her doorstep, sad and pitiful, waiting for him to return.

The teacher's voice filters through my reverie. 'You must focus on the essence, my girl. Don't let yourself be carried away by the impulsiveness of emotion and the whims of the spirit!'

But Narjiss was not listening to the teacher. I see her holding on to her son, trying to prevent him from leaving. 'I love my son more than I love myself. He is the juice of my heart, the stuff of my liver! This boy is the most beautiful thing that flutters in my breast!'

'But, sir, what if he missed her too and came back in secret to say goodbye and tell her that his disappearance was dictated by God and that he would come back to her some day? Would she believe him or would she scold him and say: "Where have you been? My heart was between my feet with worry!"' I continued in silence: *I thought a fierce monster had shredded your flesh from your bones.*

'I have one question for you, student!'

I have to tread carefully: this is the first time Ustaz Najib has called me 'student' and not 'my girl', and the space between his eyebrows was now filled with furrows, like little hills.

'Have you heard the saying: "A strong believer is more beloved to God than a weak believer"?'

'Yes, sir.'

'Now tell me: What is your favourite fruit?'

The truth was that my favourite fruits were the ones I'd never tasted before: the strawberries, pineapples and mangoes that I'd seen for sale at Souk al-Ifranj, the market frequented by foreigners. But something in my heart told me that strawberries and pineapples and mangoes would not be appropriate fruits to mention in front of Ustaz Najib, the other students or in this school in general. Figs were a safer bet: they were the cheapest and most common fruit, and had been mentioned in the Quran.

I replied that figs were my favourite, and begged God's forgiveness for not being entirely honest.

'You see, my girl? You've answered your own question. You eat figs spontaneously, unthinkingly – and this is precisely how you should soak up the True Religion, with all its wisdom and mystery: without thinking, without judgement.'

My mind drifts as I think about how I eat figs. I think of how I often admire the smoothness of their skin, their tiny ruby-red seeds. How I always split one open before putting it into my mouth to make sure the worms hadn't beaten me to it.

Before I know it my hand has shot up again and the sentences fall from my mouth, one after the other, before I've been given permission to speak.

'The thing is, Ustaz Najib, I don't eat figs unthinkingly. I think a lot about how the trees were planted, how they were nourished by the sun and rain, how the fruits grew, and how they came to be so sweet, like honey. But the Mahdi is a mystery to me. Where is he? Is it really possible for someone to disappear for all of these centuries?'

'Remember, student, that a strong believer is more beloved to God than a weak believer.'

'But the truth is, sir, I can't stop thinking about his poor mother. Imagine if you were to disappear when you were six or ten or fifteen years old. Would your mother give you up so easily? Wouldn't she search high and low until she found you?'

The class was silent. Ustaz Najib stared at me for a moment, stunned. Then he turned away, mumbling in a voice that faded to nothing: 'Let's move on to imam number . . . uh . . .'

That evening, I refused to wear the nightie, which had begun to feel like the scarecrows they use to frighten away birds in the orchards and the fields. I tore it slowly into long thin shreds and tossed them out of my bedroom window one by one, watching as they drifted to the ground.

When they handed out our final grades that year, I scanned the page looking for Ustaz Najib's mark. Imagine my surprise when I saw he had given me an A+. Still, when I heard my parents that night praying to God in gratitude for my place at the top of the class, I found myself insisting on leaving home to attend a well-known boarding school one hour away from the capital. I didn't wait for their answer and began to look for a scholarship right away.

And on my first night at boarding school, after the lights had been switched off and I heard the sound of silence instead of my father's voice chanting the *shahada*, I found myself giving whispered thanks to Mahdi.

'Mahdi, Mahdi, Mahdi – this is all because of you! If it hadn't been for your mother, I wouldn't have ended up here.' ∎

LUCY THE LIAR

Patrick deWitt

Lucien Minor's mother had not wept, had not come close to weeping at their parting. All that day he'd felt a catch in his throat and his every movement was achieved in chary degrees, as though swift activity would cause a breach of emotion. They had eaten breakfast and lunch together but neither had spoken a word, and now it was time for him to go but he couldn't step away from his bed, upon which he lay fully dressed, in coat and boots, sheepskin cap pulled low to his brow. Lucy was seventeen years old, and this had been his room since birth; all that he could see and put his hand to was permeated with the bewildering memories of childhood. When he heard his mother positing unknowable questions to herself from the scullery downstairs he was nearly overcome with sorrow. A valise stood alertly on the floor beside him.

Hefting himself from the mattress, he rose, stomping his feet three times: *stomp stomp stomp!* Gripping the valise by its swivelled leather handle, he walked downstairs and out the door, calling to his mother from the base of the steps before their homely cottage. She appeared in the doorway, lumpily squinting and clapping flour dust from her knuckles and palms.

'Is it time?' she asked. When he nodded she said, 'Well, come here, then.'

He climbed the five groaning stairs to meet her. She kissed his cheek before peering out over the meadow, scrutinizing the bank of storm clouds roiling up behind the mountain range which walled in their village. When she looked back at him, her expression was blank. 'Good luck, Lucy. I hope you do right by this Baron. Will you let me know how it turns out for you?'

'I will.'

'All right. Goodbye.'

She re-entered the cottage, her eyes fixed to the ground as she closed the door – a blue door. Lucy could recall the day his father had painted it, ten years earlier. He'd been sitting in the shade of the anaemic plum tree marking the inscrutable industries of an anthill when his father had called to him, pointing with the paintbrush, its bristles formed to a horn: 'A blue door for a blue boy.' Thinking of this, and then hearing his mother singing an airy tune from within the cottage, Lucy experienced a dipping melancholy. He dissected the purposelessness of this feeling, for it was true he had never been particularly close with his parents; or rather, they had never cared for him in the way he had wished them to, and so they'd never had an opportunity to achieve any stable partnership. He was mourning the fact that there was nothing much to mourn at all, he decided.

He elected to linger, a favoured pastime. Sitting upon his upended valise, legs intertwined fashionably, he removed his new pipe from his coat pocket, handling it with care, much in the way one holds a chick. He had purchased the pipe only the day prior; having never used one before, he took a particular interest as he filled it with the chocolate-and-chestnut-smelling tobacco. He lit a match and puffed, puffed. His head was enshrouded in fragrant smoke, and he felt very dramatic, and wished someone was watching him to witness and perhaps comment on this. Lucy was spindly and pale, bordering on sickly, and yet there was something pretty about him, too – his mouth was full, his black lashes long, his eyes large and blue. Privately he considered himself comely in an obscure but undeniable way.

He adopted the carriage of one sitting in fathomless reflection, though there was in fact no motion in his mind whatsoever. Holding the pipe head in the basin of his palm, he rotated the mouthpiece outward so that it rested between his middle and ring fingers. Now he pointed with it, here and there, for this was what the pipe-smoking men in the tavern did when giving directions or recalling a location-specific incident. A large part of the pipe's appeal to Lucy was the way it became an extension of the body of the user, a functional appendage of his person. Lucy was looking forward to pointing with his pipe in a social setting; all he needed was an audience for whom to point, as well as something to point at. He took another draw, but being a fledgling he became dizzy and tingly; tapping the pipe against the heel of his palm, the furry clump clomped to the ground like a charred field mouse, and he watched the blurred tendrils of smoke bleeding out through the shredded tobacco.

Staring up at the cottage, Lucy catalogued his life there. It had been lonely, largely, though not particularly unhappy. Six months earlier he had fallen ill with pneumonia and nearly died in his bedroom. He thought of the kindly face of the village priest, Father Raymond, reading him his last rites. Lucy's father, a man without God, came home from working the fields to find the priest in his home; he led the man out by the arm, this accomplished in a businesslike fashion, the way one shepherds a cat from the room. Father Raymond was startled to find himself treated in such a way; he watched Lucy's father's hand on his bicep, scarcely believing it.

'But your son is dying,' Father Raymond said (Lucy heard this clearly).

'And what is that to do with you? I trust you can see yourself out, now. Be a good chap and shut the door when you go.' Lucy listened to the priest's hesitant, shuffling steps. After the latch caught his father called out: 'Who let *him* in?'

'I didn't see the harm,' his mother called back.

'But who summoned him?'

'I don't know who, dear. He just came around.'

'He sniffed out the carrion, like a vulture,' said Lucy's father, and he laughed.

In the night, alone in his room, Lucy became acquainted with the sensations of death. Much in the way one shudders in and out of sleep, he could feel his spirit slipping between the two worlds, and this was terrifying but also lovely in some tickling way. The clock tower struck two when a man Lucy had never met entered the room. He was wearing a shapeless sack of what looked to be burlap, his beard trimmed and neat, brown-to-black in colouring; his longish hair was parted at the temple as though it had just been set with a brush and water; his feet were bare and he sported caked, ancient dirt running to the shin bone. He padded past Lucy's bed to sit in the rocking chair in the corner. Lucy tracked him through gummy, slitted eyes. He was not afraid of the stranger particularly, but then he wasn't put at ease by his presence, either.

After a time the man said, 'Hello, Lucien.'

'Hello, sir,' Lucy croaked.

'How are you?'

'Dying.'

The man raised a finger. 'That's not for you to say.' Now he fell silent and rocked awhile. He looked happy to be rocking, as though he'd never done it before and found it fulfilling. But then, as one troubled by a thought or recollection, his rocking ceased, his face became sombre, and he asked, 'What do you want from your life, Lucy?'

'Not to die.'

'Beyond that. If you were to live, what would you hope might come to pass?'

Lucy's thoughts were slothful, and the man's query was a restless puzzle to him. And yet an answer arrived and spilled from his mouth, as though he had no control over the sentiment: 'Something to happen,' he said.

The man in burlap found this interesting. 'You are not satisfied?'

'I'm bored.' Lucy began to cry a little after he said this, for it seemed to him a pathetic statement indeed, and he was ashamed of himself, his paltry life. But he was too weak to cry for long, and when his tears dried up he stared at the candlelight and shadows stuttering and lapping against the pale white seam where the wall met the ceiling. His soul was coming loosed when the man crossed over, knelt at the bedside, put his mouth to Lucy's ear and inhaled. And as he did this Lucy felt all the heat and discomfort leaving his body. The man exited holding his breath and walked down the hall to Lucy's parents' room. A moment later, Lucy's father suffered a coughing fit.

By dawn the colour had returned to Lucy's face, whereas his father's was paler, his eyes rimmed red where the lids sprouted lash. At dusk his father was bedridden, while Lucy took heedful steps around his room. When the sun rose the next morning, Lucy felt perfectly well other than a tenderness in his joints and muscles, and his father was dead in bed, his mouth a gory sneer, hands stiffened to claws. The undertakers came to remove the corpse and one of them slipped going down the steps, knocking Lucy's father's head against the corner of the tread. The violence of the blow was such that it punched a triangulated divot in the skull at the forehead, and yet the wound did not bleed, an oddity which the undertakers discussed and commented on in Lucy's presence. Lucy followed the trio out the door and watched as his frozen father was loaded into an unclean cart. The cart departed and the corpse rocked to and fro, as if under its own impulse. A spinning wind swooped under Lucy's nightshirt and the frost from the earth breathed coolly up his ankles. Dancing back and forth on the balls of his feet he waited for a feeling of remorse or reverence that did not arrive, not on that day or any other day, either.

In the months that followed, Lucy's mother's attitude towards him soured further. Eventually she admitted that, though she knew Lucy was not explicitly at fault, she felt him part way responsible for his father's death, as he had unwittingly transferred his illness to an otherwise healthy man, and so had struck him down before his time. Lucy wanted to speak to his mother of the visitor in the burlap sack, but he had a sense that this was something he mustn't discuss, at least not with her. The episode proved a nagging burden, however, and at night he found himself starting in his bed every time the house settled. When he could no longer bear this feeling, he sought out Father Raymond.

Lucy had no strong opinion of the Church. 'I don't know Adam from Adam,' he was fond of saying, one of many self-authored quips he felt deserved a superior audience to the lard-armed women who loitered about the fountain in the square. But there was something in Father Raymond he had responded to – a sincerity, an unpolluted empathy. Father Raymond was a moral and humane man. He followed the word of God to the letter and at night, alone in his chambers, felt the Holy Spirit coursing through his body like bird flocks. He was relieved to see Lucy in good health. In fact he was relieved to see anyone. The village was largely non-religious, and he passed full days without so much as a knock on the door. He ushered his visitor into the sitting room, setting out a tray of ancient cookies which crumbled to sand before Lucy could deliver them to his mouth. A pot of pale tea offered no palatable diversion and at last he gave up on the idea of refreshment altogether to tell the story of the stranger's visit. At the conclusion of the tale Lucy asked who the man was, and Father Raymond made an overtaxed expression.

'How would I know?'

'I was wondering if it wasn't God,' said Lucy.

Father Raymond looked doubtful. 'God doesn't travel through the night volleying disease.'

'Death, then.'

'Perhaps.' Father Raymond scratched his nose. 'Or perhaps he was a marauder. Is anything missing from the house, that you noticed?'

'Only my father.'

'Hmm,' said the priest. He picked up a cookie, which perished. He brushed the crumbs from his hands.

'The man will come again, I think,' said Lucy.

'He told you this?'

'No. But I feel it.'

'Well, there you are. Next time you see the fellow, be sure and ask his name.'

In this manner, Father Raymond did little to put Lucy's mind at ease regarding the stranger in the burlap sack; and yet he proved to be of assistance in another, unexpected way. When Lucy admitted to having no plans for his future the priest took the trouble to write letters of introduction to every castle within a hundred kilometres, the idea being that Lucy might excel as some manner of servant. These letters went unanswered save for one, penned by a man named Myron Olderglough, the majordomo of one Baron Von Aux's estate in the remote wilderness of the eastern mountain range. Mr Olderglough had been won over by Father Raymond's romantic description of Lucy as an 'unmoored soul in search of nestled safe-harbour'. (It was rumoured Father Raymond spent his friendless nights reading adventure novels, which coloured his dreams and waking life as well. Whether this was true or not is unknown; that the priest was partial to poetic turns of phrase is inarguable.) An offer of employment and terms of payment rounded out the missive. The position (Mr Olderglough assigned it the name of undermajordomo, which Lucy and Father Raymond decided was not a word at all) was lowly and the pay mirrored this but Lucy, having nothing better to do, and nowhere in the world to be, and feeling vulnerable at the thought of the man in burlap's return, embraced his fate and wrote back to Mr Olderglough, formally accepting the offer, a decision which led to many things, including but not limited to true love, bitterest heartbreak, bright-white terror of the spirit and an acute homicidal impulse.

Lucy regarded the village of Bury, resting – or collected, he thought, like leavings, debris – in the crease of the valley. It was such a scenic locality, and yet when he looked over the clustered hamlet he felt a sense of loss, a vague loathsomeness. Had he ever been anything other than an outsider here? No, is the answer. In a place famous for its propensity to beget brutish giants, Lucy by comparison was so much the inferior specimen. He couldn't dance, couldn't hold his drink, had no ambitions as a farmer or landowner, had had no close friendships growing up, and none of the local women found him worthy of comment, much less affection, save for Marina, and this had been the all too brief exception. He'd always known an apartness from his fellow citizens, a suspicion that he was not at all where he should be. When he took the position with Baron Von Aux he made the rounds to share the news and was greeted with benign matter-of-factness, rote well-wishing. His life in the village had been uneventful to the degree that his departure didn't warrant the humble energy required to birth an opinion.

Now Lucy's window was opened and his mother appeared, unspooling his bedside rug with a muscular snap of her wrists. The concentrated explosion of dust was backlit by the sun; it hung on the air awhile, and he stepped closer to witness its dreamy descent to earth. As the detritus – his own – coated his hair and shoulders, his mother noticed him and asked, 'You're still here? Won't you be late for your train?'

'There's time yet, Mother.'

She gave a quizzical look and stepped out of sight, leaving the rug to hang like a calf's tongue from the sill. Lucy considered the vacant window for a moment, then took up his valise and wrenched himself away, following the path through the trees and down the valley, towards the station.

He met a man walking in the opposite direction, a shabby satchel in one hand, makeshift walking staff in the other. The man had a field worker's complexion but wore his Sunday suit; when he saw Lucy he ceased walking, staring at Lucy's valise as though it posed some problem for him.

'Did you take the room at the Minor house?' he asked.

Lucy didn't understand at first. 'Take it? No, I'm just leaving there.'

The man relaxed. 'So the room's still available, then?'

Lucy's head banked to the side, the way a dog's does when it hears a faraway whistle. 'Who told you there was a room there?'

'The woman herself. She was putting up a notice at the tavern last night, and I happened to be stepping past.'

Lucy looked in the direction of the cottage, though he could no longer see it through the trees. When he had asked his mother where she was going the night before, she'd said she wanted to take the air.

'She seemed an honourable woman,' said the man.

'She is not dishonourable,' Lucy answered, still looking uphill.

'And you're only leaving there today, you say?'

'Just now, yes.'

In a covert voice, the man said, 'I hope you didn't find the accommodation lacking in some way.'

Lucy faced the field worker. 'No.'

'Sometimes you don't uncover the lack until it's too late. That's how it was with the last house. It was slave's rations by the end of my stay there.'

'You'll be happy at the Minors'.'

'She seemed an honourable woman,' the man repeated. 'I pray she doesn't mind my being early, but I've found it best to get a jump on these things.' He gestured at the incline. 'It's just this way, is it?'

'The path will take you there,' said Lucy.

'Well, thank you, boy. And good luck to you.' He bowed and walked on.

He was disappearing around a bend when Lucy called to him. 'Will you tell her you met me, sir? The woman of the house?'

'If that's what you want.' The man paused. 'But whom shall I say I met?'

'Tell her you met Lucy. And tell her about our conversation.'

The field worker seemed to think it an odd request, but he tipped his hat. 'Consider it done.'

As the man disappeared into the trees, Lucy was visited by an evil thought; and at the same moment the thought became whole, a rush of wind swarmed him, a column of air focused on his chest and face. It was true that at times a gust of wind was like a soundless voice commenting on some private notion or realization. Whether the wind agreed or disagreed with him, who could say. Certainly not Lucy; and neither was he much concerned about it. He continued down the hill. His mind was like a drum, a fist, a sail overflowing, pregnant with push and momentum.

At any rate, he was no longer bored.

Lucy thought he might pay a farewell visit to Marina, and headed to her house to see if she was in. There was no sign of Tor's gargantuan boots on her porch and he knocked, propping himself in the doorway as one merely happening past. But when she answered, she looked so naturally beautiful that his eyes must have betrayed his true feelings, a cleaved combination of adoration and acrimony. For her part, Marina evidently had no feeling for his being there. Pointing to his valise, she asked, 'Are you going somewhere?'

So, she wasn't even aware of his leaving. 'Yes,' he said. 'I've been summoned to the Castle Von Aux. Likely you've heard of it?'

'I haven't.'

'Are you certain? It's in the east, the high mountains – a very picturesque location, they say.'

'I've never heard of it, Lucy.' She gazed disinterestedly over his shoulder, hopeful for some diversion or another. 'What will you be doing in this very famous and picturesque castle?'

'I'm to be undermajordomo.'

'What's that?'

'It's akin to the majordomo, more or less.'

'It sounds to be less.'

'I will be working in concert with him.'

'Beneath him, that's what it sounds like.' She untied and retied her apron, fitting it snugly around her dainty waist. 'What's the wage?'

'It's a healthy wage.'

'But what is the figure?'

'Assuredly healthy. And they sent me a first-class ticket, as well.

A nice touch, I thought. They mean to keep me happy, that much is clear.' In actuality, they had sent a paltry advance, which had not quite covered a third-class ticket; he had had to take a loan from his mother for the remainder.

Marina asked him, 'How did you get this position?'

'I was assisted by the good Father Raymond.'

Smirking, she said, 'That old rag doll. He's all powdery, like a biscuit.' She laughed at this – laughed loudly, and for a long time. Lucy didn't understand how her laughter could be so blithe and enchanting when she herself was so covetous and ungenerous. Furthermore he couldn't comprehend why he felt such an overwhelming desire for someone who, it was plain enough to see, was patently rotten from the inside out.

He said, 'You can laugh at the man if you want, but he alone took it upon himself to help me. This is more than I can say for anyone else in these parts.'

Marina couldn't be bothered to take offence. She peered back into the house and seemed to be thinking of taking her leave, but Lucy wasn't ready to say goodbye just yet. Feinting, he removed his pipe and pointed its stem at the storm clouds, now tabled across the valley. 'Rain's coming,' he said. She did not look skyward but stared at the pipe.

'Since when do you smoke a pipe?' she asked.

'Somewhat recently.'

'How recently?'

'Very recently.'

A drugged mien came over her, and in a silky voice she said, 'Tor smokes cigarettes. He rolls them in one hand, like this.' She see-sawed her fingers against her thumb, her face affecting Tor's self-satisfaction and confidence. 'Did you hear he's working out the terms to Schultz's farm?'

Lucy had not, and his mind flooded with insults and epithets, for Schultz's property was the finest in Bury. And yet he held his tongue, wanting his farewell with Marina to be peaceable, not out of any magnanimity, but so that after Tor ruined her – he felt confident Tor

would ruin her – and she was once more alone, she would think of
Lucy's graciousness and feel the long-lingering sting of bitter regret.
In a sober tone, he told her, 'Good for Tor, then. That is, good for the
both of you. I hope you'll be very happy together.'

Marina was moved by the words, and she crossed over to hold
Lucy. 'Thank you, Lucy,' she said. 'Thank you.' Her hair brushed his
face and he could feel her breath against his neck. This unanticipated
contact was like a bell struck in the pit of his stomach, and he was
reminded of the time of their love affair, which took place during the
previous spring.

At the start it had consisted of much forest-walking, hand-holding
and eye-gazing. After a period of a month Marina realized Lucy
was not going to make love to her without encouragement, and she
encouraged him, and Lucy was scandalized, but not for very long
at all. They fell into a routine of daily fornication in the lush, sloping
fields below the village. Lucy was greatly relieved to be courting, at
long last, and he knew he had the makings of a faithful wife in Marina.
As they lay naked in the grass, the clouds moving bovinely over the
mountaintops, he pondered their future. How many children would
they have? They would have two children, one boy and one girl. They
would live modestly, and Lucy would become a schoolteacher or
cobbler or poet – some post which did not involve strenuous activity.
Each evening he would return to their humble home and his family
would swarm him, easing him into his chair by the fireplace. Would
he like a cup of tea? Why yes he would, and thank you so very much.
What of a scone? Well, why not? These daydreams caused in Lucy a
physical reaction, a pleasing tension that ran from his shoulders to the
undersides of his feet, toes curling in the sunshine.

His visions of this contented life were bolstered by the field
relations themselves, which he had thought were going markedly
well. But when, one afternoon, he said as much to Marina, her face
darkened. He asked her what was the matter and she told him, 'It's just
that . . . you don't have to handle me so gently, Lucy.' Soon afterwards
she sent him away, and Lucy spent heartsick months studying the

curious words with such fervour that they all but lost their meaning – and he never did deduce just what it was she wanted. What he was keenly aware of now was that Tor's hands were matted in curly brown hair gone blond from sun exposure, and that when he gripped a glass of ale it looked as though he were holding a thimble. Lucy hated Tor, and presently decided to tell a sizeable lie about him. Marina was saying her goodbyes when he said, 'But before I go I have something I need to tell you about this Tor.'

'Oh? Is that so?'

'Unfortunately it is. Most unfortunately, actually.'

She crossed her arms. 'What is it?'

He thought for a moment. When the lie came to him he clasped his hands solemnly. 'I happen to know for a fact that he is engaged to another woman in Horning.'

She laughed. 'Who told you this? It isn't true!'

'Oh, but I'm afraid that it is. Here is my reason for visiting. I'm quitting Bury forever but couldn't bear the thought of you being made a fool of.'

'Who is a fool?'

'You may do with this information what you will.'

She said, 'I think you're jealous of Tor, Lucy.'

'That is a fact, Marina. I am jealous of Tor. But more than that I am in contempt of him. For if you were mine I would never be seen gallivanting around Horning with another woman on my arm, and introducing her to all I passed as my bride-to-be. She is, I understand, several years younger than you.'

When Lucy set his mind to it, he was a most accomplished liar, that rare stripe who could convincingly relay information running contrary to reality with the utmost sincerity. He could see that Marina was beginning to take him seriously, and he pushed on, telling her, 'The dowry is said to be no trifling sum, either. In a way, you can't really blame Tor.'

'Enough, Lucy,' she said. 'Tell me it's a lie, now. Will you say that it is?'

'I wish that I could. But that's not possible, because what I'm saying is factual, and I once made a pact with you. Do you recall it?'

Her eyes fluttered and cast about; she was only half listening to Lucy. 'A pact,' she said softly.

'You asked me to always be true to you, and I swore that I would be. Oh, but you must remember, Marina. For you made the same pact yourself.'

Her eyes were hollow and doleful and she believed him completely, now. 'Lucy,' she said.

'Goodbye!' he said, and he turned to take his leave of her.

Walking away on the springy legs of a foal, he thought, *How remarkable a thing a lie is.* He wondered if it wasn't man's finest achievement, and after some consideration, decided that it was. ∎

Rae Armantrout's poetry collections include *Itself* and *Versed*, which was awarded the 2010 Pulitzer Prize for Poetry. Her work has appeared in many anthologies, including *Postmodern American Poetry: A Norton Anthology*. She is professor emeritus at UC San Diego.

Marc Bojanowski is the author of *The Dog Fighter*. His next novel, *Journeymen*, is forthcoming from Granta Books. He lives in northern California with his wife and daughter.

Molly Brodak is the author of three chapbooks and the poetry collection *A Little Middle of the Night*. Her memoir, *Bandit*, will be published in 2016.

Oliver Bullough has spent most of his working life in and around the former Soviet Union. He is the author of two books, *Let Our Fame Be Great*, which is about Chechnya, and *The Last Man in Russia*, which looks at Russia's demographic crisis, alcohol and the Soviet dissident movement. He is currently working on a book about Ukraine and international corruption.

Patrick deWitt is the author of *Ablutions* and *The Sisters Brothers*, which was shortlisted for the 2011 Man Booker Prize. 'Lucy the Liar' is an extract from his next novel, *Undermajordomo Minor*, forthcoming from Granta Books in the UK, Ecco in the US and House of Anansi in Canada. He lives in Portland, Oregon.

Wiam El-Tamami is a writer, editor and translator. In 2011 she received the Harvill Secker Young Translators' Prize for her translation of 'Gothic Night', by Mansoura Ez Eldin.

Sonia Faleiro is the author of *Beautiful Thing: Inside the Secret World of Bombay's Dance Bars* and *13 Men*, an investigation into gang rape in India. She is the co-founder of the global journalists' collective, Deca.

Angélica Freitas's poetry collections include *Rilke shake* and *Um útero é do tamanho de um punho* (*The Uterus Is the Size of a Fist*). She is also the author of a graphic novel, *Guadalupe*, illustrated by Odyr Bernardi. She lives in Brazil.

Kerry Howley is the author of *Thrown*, a *New York Times* Notable Book. Her work has appeared in the *Paris Review*, *Harper's*, *New York* magazine and elsewhere.

Greg Jackson has been a Fiction Fellow at the Fine Arts Work Center in Provincetown and at the MacDowell Colony, as well as a Henry Hoyns Fellow at the University of Virginia. His work has appeared in the *New Yorker* and the *Virginia Quarterly Review*. His first book, *Prodigals*, is forthcoming from Farrar, Straus and Giroux and Granta Books in 2016.

Daisy Jacobs is a BAFTA-winning writer and director based in London. Her Oscar-nominated short *The Bigger Picture* uses life-size animation to explore how we care for the elderly. She is currently working on her next film.

Hilary Kaplan is the translator of *Rilke Shake*, by Angélica Freitas and *Ghosts*, by Paloma Vidal. Her translations of Brazilian fiction and poetry have been featured on BBC Radio 4 and in *Modern Poetry in Translation*, the *White Review* and *Wasafiri*.

Max Pinckers is a Belgian photographer. His work is orientated towards long-term documentary projects presented as photobooks and installations such as *The Fourth Wall* and *Will They Sing Like Raindrops or Leave Me Thirsty*.

Bella Pollen is an author, journalist and travel writer who has contributed to *Vogue*, the *Spectator*, *The Times* and other publications. She is the author of five novels, including *Hunting Unicorns* and *The Summer of the Bear*. Pollen divides her time between London and the US. 'Possession' is an essay from a forthcoming collection of memoir pieces.

Alan Rossi's stories have appeared or are forthcoming in the *Atlantic*, the *Missouri Review*, the *Florida Review*, *Ninth Letter* and the *New Ohio Review*. He lives in South Carolina.

Hanan al-Shaykh is a novelist and a playwright. She is the author of several works, including *The Story of Zahra*, *Women of Sand and Myrrh*, *Beirut Blues*, *Only in London* and a memoir of her mother's life, *The Locust and the Bird*. She recently published a reimagining of some of the stories from the *Arabian Nights*, commissioned by the director Tim Supple for the theatre and performed in Toronto and Edinburgh in 2011. She lives in London.

Deb Olin Unferth is the author of the story collection *Minor Robberies*, the novel *Vacation* and the memoir *Revolution*.

Jillian Weise's books include *The Amputee's Guide to Sex*, *The Colony* and *The Book of Goodbyes*. She teaches at Clemson University.